P9-DWQ-244

AWESOME VOCABULARY

By

Becky Burckmyer

With illustrations by

Sage Stossel

CAREER PRESS
Franklin Lakes, NJ

CALGARY PUBLIC LIBRARY

APR -   2009

Copyright © 2009 by Becky Burckmyer

All rights reserved under the Pan-American and International Copyright Conventions. This book may not be reproduced, in whole or in part, in any form or by any means electronic or mechanical, including photocopying, recording, or by any information storage and retrieval system now known or hereafter invented, without written permission from the publisher, The Career Press.

Interior illustrations by Sage Stossel, 2008.

AWESOME VOCABULARY
EDITED BY JODI BRANDON
TYPESET BY EILEEN DOW MUNSON
Cover design by The DesignWorks Group
Printed in the U.S.A. by Book-mart Press

To order this title, please call toll-free 1-800-CAREER-1 (NJ and Canada: 201-848-0310) to order using VISA or MasterCard, or for further information on books from Career Press.

The Career Press, Inc., 3 Tice Road, PO Box 687,
Franklin Lakes, NJ 07417
www.careerpress.com

Library of Congress Cataloging-in-Publication Data
Burckmyer, Becky.
    Awesome vocabulary / by Becky Burckmyer : with illustrations by Sage Stossel.
        p. cm.
    Includes index.
    ISBN 978-1-60163-045-2
        1. Vocabulary. 2. English language—Grammar. 3. English language—
    Spoken English. I. Title.

PE1449.B847 2008
428.1--dc22

                                                                        2008048751

Contents

✳ + amicable

Introduction:
Welcoming a New You

Why a book to help build your vocabulary? It's not just so you can smart off to your friends, though that's certainly important. Seriously, this book is for you if, when speaking or writing, you find yourself at a loss, knowing there's a word for what you mean but unable to come up with it. It's for you if you're afraid the word you're about to use isn't the right one. And it's for you if you believe you'd approach the world differently if you knew you had an awesome vocabulary.

People can't help judging others by physical cues—how they look, what they wear, what they do, where they live. People also judge others by the way they speak and write. You want them to hear you speak, and to read what you write, with pleasure, even with respect. A good vocabulary can be a ticket to a better job, enhanced opportunities, and success with people you care about. By the same token, a poor vocabulary can relegate you to the pile of the unsuccessful and uninvited.

Remember that an improved vocabulary not only enables you to speak or write more concisely and attractively; it also makes it possible to understand the words others are using. Don't you hate trying to figure out via context or body language what somebody means? With an improved vocabulary, you won't smile delightedly if she tells you she had a **doleful** encounter with an old friend, or pull a glum face when he says his trip was **idyllic**. If this has been going on, expect an uptick in the interpersonal relations field.

This can be very useful at work, too. If your boss says, "An **enhanced** marketing capability would **obviate** the need to hire a PR consultant," are you unsure whether you're going to have a tiny marketing department and a PR consultant or beefed-up marketing and no consultant? Do you nod, smile, and dash for the dictionary hoping you won't forget the words before you can look them up? Hoping you heard them right so you can spell them? This is not a fun way to live; actually, it's very nervous-making, and you don't have to put up with it.

Awesome Vocabulary will help. If you read this book and work the simple exercises I've included to help log the new words into your permanent memory, your vocabulary will quickly improve. You'll be able to write and speak more concisely as well, using fewer but better words because you'll be able to pull out the just-right word for your purpose: You'll be able to say, "The firm is **reputable**," for example, instead of "People think well of this firm. I mean, it has a pretty good name in the business...." The right word makes you sound crisp and decisive, too, rather than rambling and roundabout. The kind of person, in fact, that people want to hire and promote.

So how are we doing so far? Thanks to a new and improved vocabulary, you're now president of General Motors and have 2,000 close friends in Facebook. What else can *Awesome Vocabulary* do for you? How about giving you a better understanding and greater enjoyment of what you read—books, magazines, online articles, you name it. I don't need to hammer the point home that it's more fun and more productive to read when you comprehend the words.

But don't take my word for it (joke). Have a look inside: There's some fun stuff going on in these pages. You'll learn snappy versions of tired old words. You'll find lists of words that sound alike but have different meanings, and words that look or sound as though they ought to mean one thing but actually mean something entirely different. I've included words that have astonishing backgrounds, and words that are just plain fun to throw around the conversation—such as **supercilious** and **berserk**, which have to do, respectively, with raised eyebrows and crazed Norse warriors who bite their shields. I'm not kidding.

You'll also find my favorite part: stories about people. The backbone of the book comprises eight short (and entertaining, I hope) stories that incorporate useful, fairly sophisticated vocabulary words. I've defined the new words in the pages immediately following—in thirds so you don't choke—and included exercises to increase your familiarity with each third. For each of the stories, the words to add to your vocabulary are in bold type. (Some words may be familiar to some readers; many are likely to be new. You may even find some new ones *not* bolded, and the context will help you define these.) Each time you complete a "story" chapter, you'll have added upward of 30 new words to your vocabulary.

Finally, in the back of the book is an alphabetical index to all the words, so you can see at a glance whether a word that interests you is included.

So what are you waiting for? The worst that can happen is that you'll learn a few new words! I really hope you like *Awesome Vocabulary* and find it useful.

✴ NOTES ON SOURCES

My sources for the definitions and pronunciation of the vocabulary words in this book include the following:

The American Heritage Dictionary of the English Language, 4th edition. Boston: Houghton Mifflin Company, 2006.

Merriam-Webster's Collegiate Dictionary, 11th edition. Springfield, Mass.: Merriam-Webster, 2003.

www.dictionary.com, which indexes more than 20 dictionaries and other authorities.

✴ PRONUNCIATION GUIDE

I've done my best to represent the pronunciation of words as simply and intuitively as possible. Two things should be mentioned:

1. The sound described as *a* is the sound of *past* or *pat*.

2. The capitalized syllables are stressed; the mark (′) indicates a secondary stress, as in ih·LOO·mih·nayte′. If two syllables are in all caps, stresses are equal, as in A·pul PIE.

WordSet I: River Denizens Cause Our Hero Profound Exasperation

Charlie had been fishing in Six Rocks River for four hours without a single bite. He was, **consequently**, tired, hot, and frustrated. He'd dedicated a vacation day to this enterprise and spent some serious money on new equipment: hip waders, a rod and reel, and a dazzling **array** of flies guaranteed to **seduce** the most **reluctant** trout. It was his first day with all the new toys, and the fish had **eluded** him. Maybe it was time to quit.

HE WAS TIRED, HOT, AND **FRUSTRATED**
THE FISH HAD **ELUDED** HIM

He **uttered** a **profound** sign and **clambered** up onto the river bank. All at once, for the first time that day, the water came alive with flipping fins and **thrashing** tails. Charlie was **flabbergasted**. "You'd think they were mocking me!" he cried in **exasperation**. He walked a few steps on the path that led to his truck, then stopped. "I'm not leaving yet. I can't let them get away with that." The afternoon was young, the sky azure, and gentle **zephyrs** ruffled the treetops. Was there anywhere else he'd rather be? he asked himself **rhetorically**.

He stepped back to the river, slid down the bank, and **recommenced** his fishing. Of course, there was now no sign of the fish, but at least he knew he was in a good spot. Time passed, and Charlie began to believe his bad luck was holding steady. He decided to give the **denizens** of the river one last chance. He flicked his line backward and **executed** a graceful cast. The fly **alit** on the water's surface, bobbed there for a second or two—then suddenly disappeared. He had a bite!

Charlie whipped the rod upward. He had it! Careful to **maintain** the **tension** on his line, he watched it zigzag as the fish swam **frantically** to and fro. It began to **gyrate** in wide **arcs**, and Charlie very gradually began to reel it in. The fish put up a **gallant** fight, but **eventually** it tired. Charlie **mustered** all his strength, lifted the **flailing** trout from the river, and scooped it into his dip net, where it **floundered**, gasping.

The fish was a beauty, 5 pounds at a minimum, with **iridescent** scales in hues of pale pink and blue, and stippled with gray in rows along its sides. Charlie **hunkered** down on the river bank to view it, **mute** with admiration. Such a catch made all the effort and **expenditures** worthwhile.

He remembered his father's **admonition**: "Never keep more than you need." **Extracting** his cell phone from his pants pocket under the hip waders, he called Marcy. "Hey, sweetie. I'm bringing home a 5-pounder! See if the Welches can come over. I'll stop for corn and a blueberry pie at the farm stand."

Expertly, Charlie gutted the trout and scraped the shining scales away. With his knife he worked to **excise** the fish's backbone. A generous trout **filet** from each side rewarded his efforts. He wrapped them in newspaper and placed them lovingly in his cooler. Humming to himself, he **assembled** his gear and **strode** up the trail to his Ford pickup. A venture that had seemed doomed to failure had been **transformed** into a **resounding** success—and he deserved full credit for the **metamorphosis**!

Charlie's Words, 1st Third

consequently (CON·suh·kwent´·lee) As a result. I spent all my money—*consequently*, I am broke. Compare *subsequently*, which means next. They went to France and *subsequently* rented a house in Spain. With consequently, there's a cause and effect relationship: I spent the money, therefore I'm penniless. With subsequently, one thing simply follows another. Consequently has a noun form as well: As a *consequence*, I am broke. And an adjective form, consequent, meaning resultant, happening because of: His illness and *consequent* retirement affected the company greatly.

array (uh·RAY) A collection or assortment, often an impressive variety. Charlie has a variety of new flies with which he hopes to catch fish. You can have an array of almost anything, from an *array* of recipes in your cooking file to an *array* of new Hondas at the sales lot. The word carries a picture of a beautiful layout, perhaps designed purposely to attract or fascinate: an *array* of colorful scarves on the counter.

seduce (seh·DOOCE, seh·DYEWCE) To lure or attract, usually with the purpose of entrapping; also, to lead astray. That's exactly what Charlie's array, above, is meant to do. Specifically, the word usually means the sort of thing sexpots do, and it's used figuratively here to describe Charlie's effort to reel in a trout; used seriously about a person, it's not really admirable (unless it's your ambition to be a sexpot).

reluctant (rih·LUK·tent) Unwilling; not wanting to cooperate. You might say you're *reluctant* to get in the middle of a fight between a husband and wife, for example. And the trout are definitely *reluctant* to take Charlie's bait, despite his seductive array of flies.

elude (ih·LOOD) To avoid or evade; to get away from. The trout are *eluding* capture; I might attempt to *elude* someone chasing me; figuratively, success might *elude* me. We apply the adjective elusive to a person or thing that keeps getting away: The Loch Ness monster (if it exists at all) is famously *elusive*.

uttered (UH·terd) The verb utter means to say, speak, or make a sound with one's voice. Charlie *utters* a sigh. You might note that someone hasn't *uttered* a word since she arrived, or that she *uttered* one or two polite sentences before she left. Interestingly, the adjective utter and adverb utterly have nothing to do with speech; they mean completely or totally: She made an *utter* mess of her room; John is *utterly* disgusted with her. Both words come from the Old English for out or outside.

profound (proe·FOUND) Deep, below the surface, intense. Often refers to emotion: My *profound* affection for Kathryn nearly made me weep. Dislike can be equally profound. There can be a *profound* gulf between my goals and my actual achievements, between my expectations and reality. Someone young and inexperienced may exhibit *profound* naivete. Charlie's sigh comes from deep inside.

clambered (KLAM·burd) The verb to clamber means to climb with effort and probably ungracefully. In other words, if I'm clambering, I probably don't look so great. And it's pretty hard work. One *clambers* over big rocks, or up into a tree that doesn't have a lot of handy branches. A fireman might *clamber* down his ladder with someone he's rescued slung over his shoulder. Not surprisingly, *clambering* up the riverbank isn't very graceful.

thrashing (THRASH·ing) To thrash is to stir or move about wildly; the fish are really putting on a show. The verb can also mean to beat, as with a stick; you can *thrash* (or thresh) grain or you can *thrash* a schoolboy (that's probably a sense stuck in the 19th century. We don't do much of that kind of thrashing any more, which is probably too bad, because some people—well, never mind).

flabbergasted (FLAB·err·gast´·ed) If you are flabbergasted, you're stunned, shocked, amazed, dumfounded, and taken by surprise. Whatever's coming down, you weren't expecting it. It's a strong word, meaning that you are truly overcome with astonishment: I'd be *flabbergasted* if they told me Madonna had run a marathon in 2:20, but I probably wouldn't be *flabbergasted* by a friend's unexpected arrival.

exasperation (egg·zass´·puh·RAY·shun) Annoyance, anger, or state of just being fed up. It's a useful verb also: If you're exasperated, you're at the end of your rope with who- or whatever. The kids *exasperate* you when they keep sticking their feet out the car window. Charlie's just about had it with these fish.

zephyrs (ZEH·furz) This word comes to us from Zephyros, the Greek god of the west wind, and it means a wind out of the west, typically (at least to the Greeks) a gentle wind. By extension, a zephyr is a soft breeze from any quarter, the kind that's always caressing the cheek of a heroine in a governess novel. You know the kind. Or not, if you're a guy. Was that sexist? The world is now safe for guys to read governess novels.

rhetorically (reh·TORR·ih·kull·ee) Rhetoric (RETT·err·ik) used to be a school subject, like math or English, concerned with effective public speaking. Rhetoric can also mean empty or insincere talk. I love Webster's definition of rhetorically: "asked merely for effect with no answer expected." If I ask *rhetorically*, "Is there no level to which my opponent will not stoop?" I don't expect anyone to answer yes or no: I'm simply making the point that the person is a slimeball.

✸ PRACTICING CHARLIE'S WORDS, 1ST THIRD

The words for the first third of Charlie's story are:

array	exasperation	seduce
clamber	flabbergasted	thrashing
consequently	profound	utter
elude	reluctant	zephyrs
	rhetorically	

A. Match the following list of adjectives with their correct definitions in the right-hand column:

1. flabbergasted   a. intense, deep
2. utter   b. total, complete
3. reluctant   c. astounded
4. profound   d. unwilling, not wishing to

B. Fill in the blanks with the correct list words:

1. I've put on my prettiest dress and drenched myself with perfume. I am trying to _____ the new man in my life.

2. I've worked hard all my life, but success always seems to _____ me.

3. I demanded _____, "With a friend like you, who needs enemies?"

4. My attempts to improve the unpleasant child's manners ended in _____.

5. I had no breakfast and was _____ starving when lunchtime arrived.

6. The fashion house's beautiful models showed off a dazzling _____ of formal wear.

7. The prevailing winds in Patagonia are surely not _____.

C. If I *clamber* up a cliff, I probably look _____.

1. graceful   3. awkward
2. busy   4. dignified

D. An antonym is the opposite of a word. Choose the word that's the closest antonym for *thrashing*.

1. grouchy   3. tidy
2. outgoing   4. still

E. Complete the following story with list words.

Although I was (unwilling) to (climb) up the tree, it seemed the best way to (avoid) capture. My pursuers were angry, and I (as a result) was feeling (deep) discomfort. "How did I get into this mess?" I asked (without expecting a reply). In my (complete) (frustration) I began (flailing wildly) around in the tree. I heard a noise below and looked down to see an (assortment, group) of childish faces gazing up, (astounded). "Come on down, Mister," said a little boy. "Those people have given up and left. You're safe now!"

Answers

A. 1. c; 2. b; 3. d; 4. a
B. 1. seduce; 2. elude; 3. rhetorically; 4. exasperation; 5. consequently; 6. array; 7. zephyrs
C. 3
D. 4
E. reluctant; clamber; elude; consequently; profound; rhetorically; utter; exasperation; thrashing; array; astounded

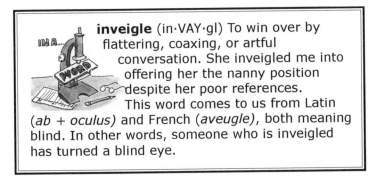

inveigle (in·VAY·gl) To win over by flattering, coaxing, or artful conversation. She inveigled me into offering her the nanny position despite her poor references.
This word comes to us from Latin (*ab* + *oculus*) and French (*aveugle*), both meaning blind. In other words, someone who is inveigled has turned a blind eye.

Charlie's Words, 2nd Third

denizens (DEN·ih·zens) Residents; inhabitants; those who live in a certain place. The word can also mean someone who just hangs out, a regular: the *denizens* of Maggie's Pool Parlor, for instance. The word comes from Latin *de*, from, and *intus*, within—hence, a person from within. It's a more colorful word than residents or inhabitants, and as such deserves to be used.

executed (EX·ih·kyoot´·ed) To execute means to do, fulfill, or perform: It's what executives do. Also ballerinas: She *executed* a brilliant *grand jeté.* It's a good word that can impart a glow of sophistication to your prose. If you knew it up until now as only as a word for killing a criminal, good: Your horizons are expanding.

alit (uh·LITT) To alight is to descend or land. The plane *alit* on the runway. You can also say the plane alighted—either's correct. Birds *alight* on telephone wires. Airborne seeds *alight* far from the original plant. The word has a sense of, well, lightness and gracefulness, like a dragonfly. You wouldn't say a hippopotamus swam over and *alit* on the island: The critter is too clumsy and heavy.

maintain (mane·TANE) To continue, keep up. I usually *maintain* a steady speed of 65 mph on the highway. You can also maintain a car, in the sense of keeping it in good running order; and you can maintain a position in a discussion or argument: Sally *maintained* that Justin had only been trying to help when he upset the milk. Charlie *maintains* a tight line to keep the fish from working the hook out of its mouth.

tension (TENN·shun) State of being tight, in an actual or figurative sense. Charlie keeps his line tight; tension is also the feeling of tightness you get in times of emotional strain. And you can use the word to mean friction between people: There's a lot of *tension* within Brad's family over the will.

frantically (FRANN·tih·kull·ee) In a frenzy, desperately, in a frantic manner, frantic meaning half-crazy with emotion, usually negative emotion. I searched *frantically* for my missing wallet. The fish, fighting for its life, is understandably moving in a mood of wildly negative emotion.

gyrate (JYE·rate´) To revolve, to turn in circles. The fish is literally swimming in circles. The word can be used figuratively: I studied for the math exam so hard that numbers *gyrated* in front of my eyes all night. The prefix *gyro-* means spinning. This prefix also helps compose the word gyroscope: You may have owned or seen a toy gyroscope, which sits on a base and spins at improbable angles.

arcs (ARKS) An arc is a segment of a circle, such as a rainbow or an eyebrow. Charlie's fish is attempting to escape by swimming back and forth, describing *arcs* in the water. If you're a good skater, you can carve *arcs* on the ice. The word comes from the Latin *arcus*, meaning bow, as in bow and arrow. Interestingly, its homonym, ark, comes from a different root entirely. Ark, meaning a large, heavy boat, comes from the Latin word *arca*, which means chest or heavy box.

gallant (GA·lunt) Brave; extra courteous, especially to women. I notice that people use the word gallant to mean brave when the outcome isn't going to be good: She put up a *gallant* fight against cancer, for example, may be written in an obituary. And Sir Walter Raleigh was *gallant* when he spread his cloak over the puddle to spare Queen Elizabeth I's shoes, despite the fact that the outcome for the cloak was dim.

eventually (ee·VEN·choo·al·ee) At some time in the future; finally. In this case, we're talking finally: The fish at last gets tired. You may defer going to college, but *eventually* you'll get there. The adjective is eventual: The biography never mentions his *eventual* marriage to Selena.

mustered (MUSS·ter) To muster means, among other things, to gather or collect, to bring to bear. I needed to *muster* all my resources to deal with Esther. Charlie brings all his strength to bear on the project of landing the trout. The word can also mean to assemble or gather together, as troops: We *mustered* as many volunteers as possible for the bikeathon. If you're discharged from the military, you *muster* out. Oddly, a flock of peacocks is called a *muster*.

flailing (FLALE·ing) To flail means to move around violently or erratically, to lash out. See *thrashing*, page 12; the two words share an element of meaning. Charlie's fish is twisting and writhing in its effort to escape. I *flailed* away with the swatter in an effort to scare away the flies. Flail can also mean to beat or strike: I *flailed* the water in my effort to stay afloat. And flail is a noun: A *flail* is an old tool for separating grain from stalks.

iridescent (ihr´·rih·DESS·nt) Colored like the rainbow. In Greek mythology, Iris was the goddess of the rainbow. Her name will remind you not to double the r. Oil can leave *iridescent* pools; mother-of-pearl is *iridescent*. The trout's scales are of rainbow colors.

☀ PRACTICING CHARLIE'S WORDS, 2ND THIRD

The words for the second third of Charlie's story are:

alit	execute	iridescent
arcs	flailing	maintain
denizens	frantically	mustered
eventually	gallant	tension
	gyrate	

A. Synonyms are words with the same or nearly the same meaning. Which list word is the closest synonym for *spin*?

B. Which sentence uses the word *gallant* correctly?

1. I didn't like the gallant fishing gear he brought with him: It was out of date.

2. He sent a gallant e-mail telling me he could no longer stand my nagging.

3. Your gallant response, that I might call you at midnight if necessary, meant a lot to me.

4. The river looks especially gallant today with the sun glittering on its surface.

C. Fill in the blanks with the correct list words:

1. The Common with its bandstand was beautiful, a special place to the _____ of the town.

2. I don't know how you think I can _____ a decent standard of living on this salary.

3. The golden eagle was making great swooping _____ in the sky above the terrified rabbit.

4. I signaled _____ to the train to stop, but the engineer didn't respond.

5. The skier proceeded to _____ a series of incredibly tight turns.

6. I thought June would never stop talking, but _____ she ran out of funny stories.

D. Ran is to sit as flew is to _____.

E. Which word is related to an old-fashioned threshing device?

F. Choose the correct definition for the following list words:

1. tension
   a. tightness, emotional stress   c. pain
   b. ability   d. weight

2. iridescent
   a. shining   c. unusual, exotic
   b. composed of many colors   d. slimy

3. mustered
   a. seasoned, spiced   c. made possible
   b. gathered, pulled together   d. dealt with

G. Complete the following story with list words:

I could feel the (stress) in my shoulders as I entered the rink to (perform) my skating program. The first skater had made a (brave) effort, but had fallen; the second did little but (twirl) (wildly) in increasing (pieces of circle). If I could (keep) my lead, I could win. I (gathered) my courage and began. My (rainbow-colored) costume fluttered as I leaped and (finally) (landed). The applause burst forth: I had won!

Answers

A. gyrate

B. 3

C. 1. denizens; 2. maintain; 3. arcs; 4. frantically; 5. execute; 6. eventually

D. alit

E. flailing

F. 1. a; 2. b; 3. b

G. tension; execute; gallant; gyrate; frantically; arcs; maintain; mustered; iridescent; eventually; alit

Charlie's Words, 3rd Third

hunkered (HUNK·erd) To hunker is to crouch, sit, or settle down on one's haunches. The word can carry a sense that the person who's hunkering may stay put for a while. In this case, Charlie's just squatting to clean the fish. But if I *hunker* down in the comfortable chair by your fireside, I may be unwilling to leave. We say someone's hunkered down in his cabin for the winter.

mute (MYOOT) Unable to speak or choosing not to speak; making no sound. I was *mute* with horror at Agnes's words. It's used here as a figure of speech, not literally: Charlie is struck dumb, figuratively, by the beauty of the fish. As you probably know, the mute button on your remote or your phone shuts off the sound. A mute is a person who doesn't speak; it can also be a device to dampen or tone down the sound of a musical instrument.

expenditures (ex·SPEN·dih·chers) Expense; money or resources outlaid. You can talk about expenditures of energy or time as well as money: The fund-raiser represents a huge *expenditure* of energy. The word can be singular or plural: After a multiple microburst hit our house, we incurred many *expenditures* for its repair. The verb expend means to spend or lay out: we're going to *expend* all our resources to make Sharon's wedding beautiful.

admonition (add´·moh·NIH·shun) A mild criticism or reproach: The children felt bad about teasing the cat and were embarrassed by Angus's *admonition*. An admonition can also mean a warning, as Charlie's father gave him, or advice to prevent something bad happening: You ignored my *admonition* against skating on the pond, and now you're pretty wet. To admonish means to reproach or warn someone.

extracting (ex·TRACT) If you extract something, you draw it forth, as information, or pull it out, as a tooth. The detectives were busy *extracting* the name and address of the alleged killer's wife. Extracting is often done with effort: Dressed in hip waders, Charlie probably has to fumble around in his pocket before he's able to get his cell phone out.

excised (ek·SIZED) To excise literally means to cut out. We use it as we'd use remove or take out. It's definitely a $50 word: You wouldn't say, "I *excised* the pit from my peach." In novels, people are always trying to *excise* terrible memories. A surgeon tries to *excise* cancerous tissue.

filet (fill·LAY) A tender, boneless cut of meat, fish, or poultry I'm sure you've encountered on menus, the *filet* mignon being probably the best known. Here our hero has created his own fish filets.

assembled (ah·SEM·buld) To assemble means to collect, to bring, or to put together, so assembled means brought or put together: Camping gear is often *assembled*. The word can also be used without an object: people can simply *assemble*, in a courtyard or under the clock at Grand Central Station.

strode (STRODE) This is the past form of the verb to stride, which means to walk with long steps, or strides. The word has an overtone of walking or marching purposefully. If I'm striding, I'm not just out for air; I'm trying to get somewhere, often in a hurry. That's the way Charlie's walking. Stride, usually plural, can also mean progress: We are making great *strides* in our fight against malaria.

transformed (tranz·FORMD) Changed, altered, converted. Charlie's day has changed for the better. Transformed can also mean changed for the worse: My charming date had suddenly been *transformed* into a grumbling, whining creep.

resounding (ree·ZOWN·ding) To resound means to be filled with sound, or to sound or reverberate loudly. The concert hall *resounded* with shouts of applause. By extension the word also means definite or emphatic: there's no question that Charlie's day was a success. We may also say a proposal went down to *resounding* defeat in Town Meeting, meaning it didn't just lose: It lost big-time.

metamorphosis (met´·ah·MORE·fuh·siss) A change or transformation. A tadpole undergoes a *metamorphosis* and becomes a frog. Jenny had undergone a *metamorphosis* while I was away and became a beautiful woman. Because Charlie didn't give up, he earned the positive change that took place at the end of his day.

✸ PRACTICING CHARLIE'S WORDS, 3RD THIRD

The words for the last third of Charlie's story are:

admonition	extracting	mute
assembled	filet	resounding
excised	hunkered	strode
expenditures	metamorphosis	transformed

A. Fill in the blanks with the correct list words:

   1. The dentist laughed unpleasantly while
      _____ my tooth.

   2. I called Tootsie, but the big dog just _____
      down beside his new friend the cat.

   3. After three hours with the makeup lady, Tessa was
      _____ into a serious beauty.

   4. The boxer dealt his opponent a _____ blow
      to the jaw.

B. Which word is the closest synonym for *strode*?

   1. walked quickly   3. danced

   2. stamped   4. delayed

C. What has taken place when a gawky teenager becomes an
   elegant young person?

D. Choose the word that's the closest antonym for *mute*.

   1. attractive   3. talkative

   2. bitter   4. busy

E. If I am worried about *expenditures*, what am I least likely
   to do?

   1. Take out a Costco membership

   2. Start a home baking business

   3. Buy a new car

   4. Return that new outfit to Lord & Taylor

F. Match the list words with their correct definitions in the right-hand column:

1. assembled	a. mild reproach
2. filet	b. got together
3. admonition	c. cut out
4. excised	d. boneless meat

G. Complete the following story with list words:

I (crouched) down on the boat deck, almost (speechless) with fatigue. Harry (walked purposefully) to the stern. I told him we were all too tired to eat aboard, but he replied with a (loud, reverberating) "Nonsense!" Despite my (warning), he (removed) the internal organs, (cut out) the bone from the fish, and carved out the tasty (boneless piece of meat) from each side. Of course, the children (gathered) to watch as he (changed) the fish into a meal. Oh well, I thought, bluefish for the seven of us is one way to control (financial resources outlaid).

Answers

A. 1. extracting; 2. hunkered; 3. transformed;
4. resounding

B. 1

C. metamorphosis

D. 3

E. 3

F. 1. b; 2. d; 3. a; 4. c

G. hunkered; mute; strode; resounding; admonition; extracted; excised; filet; assembled; transformed; expenditures

The Right Word: Write Quite Right, Not Almost Right

This chapter deals with words that are easily confused, because they either sound alike or share an element of meaning. Please believe me when I say it is a very important chapter. Close is by no means good enough if you are aiming for an awesome vocabulary! The following pairs of words contain a word that is *exactly* right for your purpose and one that's not quite right. Scrutinize these pairs carefully and mark any definitions you don't already know. This will help you recognize and choose the just-right word every time. Note that wherever possible I've included memory helpers, known as mnemonic devices—remember "I before E, except after C"? That's a mnemonic device—to help you differentiate between right on and wrong.

ability   skill

capacity   potential ability

The two words don't mean quite the same thing. Your *ability* refers to something you've learned how to do—the ability to swim a mile, for example; your *capacity* refers to an innate talent.

> I'm amazed at his *ability* to hold his breath for four minutes.

> Jerry has an amazing *capacity* for learning languages.

∗

adapt   to adjust; to develop a suitability to the situation or environment

adopt   to take on characteristics; to take as one's own, like an *adopted* child

Suzanne has *adapted* well to the new school system.

Although he loved his *adopted* country, he never forgot his native Russia.

✳

adverse   not good; unfavorable; usually used in reference to an inanimate object

averse   unwilling; disinclined; usually used in reference to a person

I think he's having an *adverse* reaction to Cream of Wheat.

I'm *averse* to sharing my Color Me Beautiful chart.

✳

affect, v.   to cause an effect; to induce a feeling

effect, v.   to make happen; to cause

The bad weather *affected* Dora: She cried for a week.

You seem to think I can *effect* miracles with those foul twins of yours.

How to distinguish between these two verbs? Their functions are alphabetical in this sentence:

If you're *affected* by your worries, you must *effect* a solution.

Three other uses of *affect* and *effect* follow.

affect, v.   to feign; to adopt falsely

Daphne *affects* the manners of a Southern gentlewoman every Derby Day.

affect, n.   to psychologists, a term for mood

Patrick's *affect* seems pleasant but blunted; he shows very little emotion of any kind.

effect, n.   result

The morphine had a frightening *effect*: hallucinations of tremendous force and variety.

✳

afflict to cause to suffer

inflict (on) to impose or force (on)

These words are not synonyms, though they share a shade of meaning. Here's how to use them correctly:

> Sherri has been *afflicted* with Lyme disease since July 2006.

> The hurricane *inflicted* major damage on Highway 109.

✴

alternate happening by turns; every other

alternative offering a choice

> Beth carpools for me on *alternate* Thursdays.

> We can leave; an *alternative* approach would be to ask Michael to leave.

Alternative can also mean unconventional: an *alternative* lifestyle.

✴

ambiguous hazy or unclear; capable of different interpretations

ambivalent unsure; indecisive; holding different opinions at different times

Note that a thing or idea is *ambiguous*; a person feels *ambivalent*.

> The wording of the will is *ambiguous*; we need more lawyers!

> I'm afraid Charlotte's father is *ambivalent* about her marriage to Walter.

✴

Please Don't Say That!
jewelry (JOO·el·ree, JOOL·ree) The dictionary never heard of JOOL·uh·ree. I'm sorry to say I have. Please don't pronounce it that way.

---

among   in the midst of three or more things

between   in the middle of two things

> Don't be frightened: You are *among* friends.

> *Between* Betty and Veronica, I can't decide who should be my prom date.

This rule is pretty reliable; however, there's an exception. If business of whatever sort is being conducted between each pair of three or more persons or things, you may, in fact you should, use *between*. The standard example is negotiations between countries:

> A truce *between* Russia, France, and China held for more than 10 years.

Russia and France had a truce; Russia and China had—well, you get the idea.

✳

amount   quantity; how many: used for what cannot be individually counted

number   quantity; how many: used for individually countable items

I have a huge *amount* of pocket change; I have a huge *number* of pennies, nickels, and dimes. That's the difference. If you can't count something—be it fog or bitterness or household cleanser—the word you want is *amount*. Helpful hint: *Amount* is usually used with singular nouns, *number* with plural nouns. Not hard.

> It's hard to calculate the *amount* of *damage* done by the storm as opposed to the looters.

> My brother had a *number* of unsavory *companions* he never brought home to meet Mother.

✳

as   similar to; precedes a verb

like   similar to; precedes a noun

The rule is that *like* precedes a noun (or pronoun).

The snow fell *like a thick white blanket* on the fields.

He looks *like an angel* sleeping in his crib.

Like a blanket, an angel, a lead balloon—if a noun follows the word, then the word should be *like*.

As, on the other hand, precedes a verb. In fact, it usually precedes a complete sentence with a subject and verb.

As Judith pointed out, we need to decide before Thursday.

As planned, the F-22 Raptors did a flyover. (A verb in this case, although not a complete sentence. The verb must be there.)

This rule means that the dreadful expression "Like I said" is **always** incorrect. Don't let me catch you saying it, let alone writing it. The verb that follows, *said*, means the correct word is *as*: *As I said*.

While we're on the subject of *like*, I have two more rules. Don't use *like* as a substitute for *as if* or *as though* in writing.

No: You look *like* you're lost.

Yes: You look *as if* you're lost.

No: The ship looks *like* it's aground.

Yes: The ship looks *as though* it's aground.

Although you'll probably get away with it in conversation, because conversation is written on air, *like* isn't strictly correct here, because the word is meant to suggest similarity, and *you* are not similar to *you're lost* any more than the ship is similar to *it's aground*. In writing, which can easily sit around and make you look bad, *as if* is the wiser choice.

And one final restriction on *like*: Don't use it if you can substitute *such as*.

No: We bought spring flowers, *like* daffodils and
         tulips, to decorate the tables.

Yes: We bought spring flowers, *such as* daffodils
         and tulips, to decorate the tables.

No: He did a lot of stupid things, *like* toasting the flower girl instead of the bride.

Yes: He did a lot of stupid things, *such as* toasting the flower girl instead of the bride.

Although *like* does indeed imply similarity, the connection is inexact. *Such as* more accurately expresses the notion that what will follow is an example of what went before.

Try my simple test: If you've written *like* and aren't sure it's correct, try substituting *as*, *as if*, and *such as*. If one sounds better than like, by all means use it. Here's an example:

Marjorie is so much *like* her sister it kind of scares me.

Here we go: She looks *as* her sister? Ew. She looks *as if* her sister? As if her sister what? She looks *such as* her sister? Not a chance. So you can be sure plain old *like* is correct.

Let's try another:

People who need extra time to take their seats, *like* people in wheelchairs or those with small children, may board the aircraft now.

> **You Try It!**
>
> Fill in the blanks with the proper "like" word(s).
>
> Joann fell sideways, _____ she had been hit on her left shoulder.
>
> When the smoke cleared, there sat Marty smiling _____ the Cheshire Cat.
>
> _____you predicted, the company overextended itself and is bankrupt.
>
> She has a genius for math, just _____ her father.
>
> Camping gear, _____sleeping bags and tents, is surprisingly inexpensive.
>
> [Answers: as if, like, As, like, such as]

As people in wheelchairs? Doesn't sound so good, and there's no verb following. *As if* people in wheelchairs? Nonsense. *Such as* people in wheelchairs? Now you're talking. *Such as* is correct.

✳

assume   to believe or suppose

presume   to take to be fact without proof

Both words have many meanings, but these are the two that overlap and can be confused. Remember that *pre-* means (among other things) *before*. Therefore, *presume* has the meaning of making a judgement before knowing all the facts.

> I *assume* Rick will be here by noon; at least, he was planning on it.

> I had *presumed* she wanted to meet the author also, but she wanted to leave.

✳

beside   next to; close to

besides   also; in addition to

> *Beside* the bed sat a little table with a pitcher and a lamp.

> But Nelson doesn't need two bikes, and *besides*, it isn't fair!

✳

bring   to carry toward

take   to carry away from; to carry to another place

I'm not sure why this comes up all the time. It seems pretty obvious: Bring it here; take it there. But my writing classes always mention it, so somebody must be doing it wrong.

> Be a dear and *bring* me my whip, would you?

> Please *take* all your belongings when you leave the aircraft.

✳

can   am/is/are able to

may   am/is/are allowed to

Of course you *can* stroll downtown in your birthday suit. But you *may* not, or not without consequences. Don't use *can* if you're talking about permission.

No: Cool! John says Bella *can* borrow his camcorder.

Yes: John says Bella *may* borrow his camcorder.

No: *Can* I put Mrs. Wilson's ferret in the dryer?

Yes: *May* I put Mrs. Wilson's ferret in the dryer?

✳ '

censor   to delete selectively; to cut out

censure   to criticize sharply

We need to *censor* our Cinco de Mayo video before Johnny watches it.

Craig was *censured* for his part in hoisting Mr. Gray's car onto the roof.

✳

climactic   concerning the climax, or high point

climatic   concerning the climate, or typical weather conditions

If you're talking about climate change, don't let that second *c* get into your pronunciation. Likewise, be sure to include it if you're talking dramatic moments. Otherwise, you can pick up an amateur writer or speaker label easily.

At the *climactic* scene, Lady Macbeth enters, sleepwalking.

Normal *climatic* variations would account for some of the melting ice.

✳

compare to   to suggest a similarity between two things

compare with to observe similarities and differences between two things

When they saw my new body, they *compared me to* Hercules.

Compared with his other books, James Patterson's new book is slow and dull.

✳

compose	to make up; to form
comprise	to include; to be composed of; also, but not always acceptably, to compose

Comprise is increasingly used to mean *compose*. Strict grammarians and people who care about word usage frown on this. I hear about it quite a lot. My take, as usual, is why get into it? Why not just say *compose* if you mean compose? Be aware that *comprise* has that special meaning of including and that you may offend a picky person (or several) if you use it as a synonym for *compose*.

> Four sections *compose* this unusual piece of music.

> This unusual piece of music *comprises* four sections.

✳

continual	repeated; over and over
continuous	steady; uninterrupted

> The *continual* ringing of the phone keeps me from getting any work done.

> I love the *continuous* trill of the little frogs on a spring night.

It's easy to remember which one to use: The *a* in *continual* stands for *again and again*; the *ous* in *continuous* stands for *one uninterrupted sequence*.

✳

credible	convincing; worthy of being believed; opposite of *incredible*
credulous	easily convinced; gullible; the opposite is *incredulous*

A **story** is *credible* or not. A **person** who naively trusts everything he or she hears is *credulous*.

> Shackleton and his men endured hardships that are scarcely *credible*.

> Our daughter is so *credulous* I fear she'll marry some no-count count in Italy.

✳

denote   to signify or indicate directly

connote   to suggest; to evoke

Denote is the specific word, *connote* the associative: Mother *denotes* one's female birth parent; mother *connotes* images and memories of warmth and unconditional love.

> Molly's broad, genuine smile *denoted* her pleasure in seeing Herbert.

> To me, the beach *connotes* sunny days of endless leisure, paperback fiction, and sand in the sandwiches.

✳

discreet   careful; wise; restrained

discrete   distinct from one another; countable

Don't be fooled if you see these being misused in the print media: It's been happening with discouraging frequency lately. These words do not mean the same thing.

> A nanny must be *discreet*, as she hears all kinds of family secrets.

> A series of *discrete* fundraising events, rather than one huge effort, funds the Cockapoo Rescue Program each year.

✳

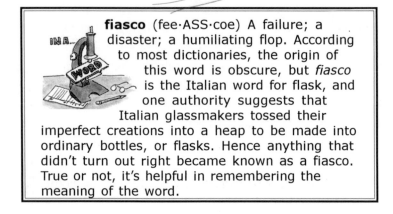

fiasco (fee·ASS·coe) A failure; a disaster; a humiliating flop. According to most dictionaries, the origin of this word is obscure, but *fiasco* is the Italian word for flask, and one authority suggests that Italian glassmakers tossed their imperfect creations into a heap to be made into ordinary bottles, or flasks. Hence anything that didn't turn out right became known as a fiasco. True or not, it's helpful in remembering the meaning of the word.

disinterested impartial; without a stake in

uninterested not interested; indifferent

Some people use them interchangeably to mean not interested, and there's good support for this position, as the words have traded meanings back and forth over many years. But it's useful, as many dictionaries do, to reserve the word *disinterested* to mean evenhanded or impartial, like a good Supreme Court Justice, and use *uninterested* to mean apathetic.

> Shouldn't a *disinterested* party act as a go-between in our dispute?

> I can't understand why all of you seem so *uninterested* in my research on Cockney rhyming slang.

✳

emigrate to leave one's native country

immigrate to come to a new country

Emigrants and immigrants work the same way. It's mostly a matter of emphasis: If you're emigrating, chances are 100 percent you are, or are about to be, immigrating.

> The potato famine in Ireland caused huge numbers of people to *emigrate*.

> Roger dreamed of *immigrating* to the United States and playing basketball.

✳

enormity great evil

enormousness great size

Although wickedness is the first meaning of *enormity*, most dictionaries give the meaning of great size as well, especially if whatever it is big enough to inspire terror. I just want you to know that its primary sense is of horrendous evil.

> The *enormity* of Claudius's act makes him unable to pray.

> Because of his *enormousness*, he needed two seats on the plane.

✳

ensure   to guarantee; to make sure

insure   to buy or sell an insurance policy

Here's your mnemonic device (memory aid): *Insure* refers to *in*surance.

> We must *ensure* that no one sees Nora before she jumps out of the cake.

> Thank goodness we had *insured* Larissa's toes before *Swan Lake*.

✳

evoke   to bring to mind; to call forth

invoke   to raise; to call up

> The smell of peonies always *evokes* memories of home.

> I *invoked* every deity of lost causes to help in my effort to clean up Agent Hart's language before the pageant.

✳

exceedingly   to a great extent; very much

excessively   too much

> Although *exceedingly* intelligent, he was awkward and ill at ease.

> Oscar Wilde grew *excessively* fat in jail.

✳

explicit   expressed; stated

implicit   implied; suggested

> He gave us an *explicit* warning not to climb over the fence.

> Behind his warning was the *implicit* fear that we'd meet up with the bull.

Implicit can also mean complete, unreserved.

> I have *implicit* faith in her ability to cope with Brian.

✳

farther   literally more distant

further   figuratively more; to a greater degree

Some dictionaries don't make this distinction; I think it's worthwhile.

> I dared not go *farther* along the gloomy hallway.

> Efforts to pry *further* into his unpleasant past made me almost ill.

✳

fewer   not as many; applies to separate items that can be counted

less   not as many; applies to an amount rather than separate items

> Edward owns *fewer* properties than Maude but has a bigger stock portfolio.

> I own **less** real estate than my brother and sister.

✳

flaunt   to show off or parade

flout   to disregard; to scorn

A lot of people mix these up—maybe because you can imagine the same kind of person doing both?

> I can't stand to watch Frances *flaunt* her new wealth at the casino.

> She *flouted* convention by wearing her bathing suit to church.

✳

flounder   to be in trouble; to thrash helplessly

founder   to collapse; to sink

Both of these may be used literally or figuratively: You may *flounder*, then *founder*, in a swimming pool or in a new business venture.

> I watched as Howard *floundered* in the mud, but I realized he didn't want my help.

The partnership *foundered* because Jake and Tess didn't really trust one another.

✳

imply   to suggest; to indicate indirectly

infer   to figure out; to deduce

A lot of people get these confused. Don't be like them. Because *imply* comes before *infer* in alphabetical order, it's easy to remember that first, someone *implies*, and second, someone *infers* from what was implied.

The size of his house *implies* Harvey is doing all right.

I *inferred* from Chris's terse reply that I had offended him.

✳

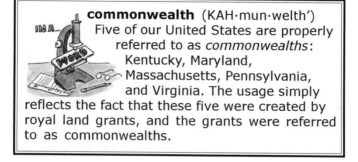

commonwealth (KAH·mun·welth´) Five of our United States are properly referred to as *commonwealths*: Kentucky, Maryland, Massachusetts, Pennsylvania, and Virginia. The usage simply reflects the fact that these five were created by royal land grants, and the grants were referred to as commonwealths.

ingenious   bright; inventive

ingenuous   trusting; naïve; honest

These words are properly applied to both persons and things: The inventor was *ingenious*; his *ingenious* invention worked. The *ingenuous* girl gave an *ingenuous* response.

What an *ingenious* way to peel chestnuts!

A bright-eyed, *ingenuous* young man from a tiny town in Idaho, he little dreamed how jaded one can become in New York City.

✳

intelligent   smart; bright; capable of learning

intellectual   interested in things of the mind; deeply into learning

Heaven knows you're *intelligent*: Why don't you use your brain?

Don's *intellectual* conversation went right over Sam's head.

✳

libel   to write or print a false accusation that damages someone's reputation

slander   to utter false words that damage a person's reputation

The distinction here is in the written versus the spoken word. Fun with mnemonics: Slander begins with an s, as does say, whereas libel resembles label, which is written.

✳

lie   to lie down

lay   to put something down

If I had a dime for every time someone has said *lay* to me when it should have been *lie*, I'd be on the Riviera right now. Don't do this: It is substandard English that brands you as unlearned. Here's how these two verbs work.

To lie: I lie; I lay; I have lain; lying

If you lie, you lie *down*: You move from a vertical to a horizontal position. This word doesn't take an object. In other words, you don't lie *something*. You just...lie there.

Don't *lie* on the bed in your good clothes.

She *lay* on the floor helpless, her back in spasm.

The dog *has lain* by his master's grave for a week.

The book *lying* on the hall table is for you.

To lay: I lay; I laid; I have laid; laying

This is the verb to use if you are putting *something* down: a book, a case of drinks, the bride you just carried over the threshold.

I'd better *lay this Stop & Shop bag* down if we're going to be talking for a while.

She *laid a warm blanket* over the sleeping child.

David *has laid out his cold-weather clothes* to pack for the trip.

Laying bricks for the new courtyard, the mason was enjoying his work.

The Reverend Henry Ward Beecher
Called the hen a most elegant creature;
The hen, pleased with that,
Laid an egg in his hat,
And thus did the hen reward Beecher.

You can see that, in every example, the subjects are letting something go out of their hands. If you can't point to a similar something in your sentence, the word should be lie, not lay.

✷

literally truly; actually

figuratively *not* literally, but for purposes of description

Manderley literally burned to the ground—or was it Thornfield?

We used to put iodine and baby oil all over our bodies and figuratively burn ourselves to a crisp.

As you can see, *literally* has a specific meaning, so don't use it as an intensifier. It isn't a synonym for *really*. Your readers or hearers will think you are a figurative whiffle ball if you claim to be *literally eating crow* or *talking turkey*. These are *figures of speech* and are used *figuratively*.

✷

may linking verb used in present or future

might linking verb used for past time

She *may* come over after lunch if there's time.

We hoped he *might* share his beer bread recipe
with us.

It's a grave mistake to mix up your tenses by saying, for example, "My cousin was so hairy, everyone suspected he may be a werewolf." If everyone *suspected*, it's *might*. If everyone *suspects*, on the other hand, it should be *may*.

Might may also be used in the present, however, if you are implying doubt.

Kristin *says* she *might* come to graduation if she can
get a sitter.

✳

mélange   a mixture of people or items; a mixed bag

ménage   a domestic arrangement; a household

Two useful French words that are often confused. If you're going to use them, be sure you've got the right one. *Ménage* is familiar as part of *ménage a trois*, a threesome of two men and a woman or two women and a man living as man/men and wife/wives.

Dinner was a *mélange* of beef tenderloin, cereal, and
Chinese takeout.

The Harrison *ménage*, with all those cats, makes me
break out in a rash.

✳

militate   to operate (against)

mitigate   to lessen

Jan's native intelligence *militates* against your
suggestion she's scheming to walk up the outside of
the Empire State Building.

Your company, not to mention your homemade
soup, *mitigated* my unhappiness in the hospital
waiting room.

✳

partially   not completely or altogether; a work in progress

partly   in part

The scrolls were *partially* translated by a Sanskrit scholar in the late 19th century.

My garden is composed *partly* of annuals, *partly* of dirt: The perennials never came up.

✳

pedal   to push the pedals of a machine (a bicycle, piano, etc.)

peddle   to push or sell merchandise

Pedaling the old sewing machine, I thought of my grandmother.

After a brief career in the movies, he ended up *peddling* insurance.

✳

principal   n., money accumulated debt-free, as distinct from interest

   n., head; chief person

   n., head of school

   adj., of first importance

principle   n., ethical consideration; rule of behavior

She has more than $4 million in *principal* but won't spring for a new light bulb.

The *principal* at I. Ketcham & U. Cheatham says he will take the case against the pig.

Your father and I did some time in the *principal's* office after the fire.

I believe she cited boredom as the *principal* cause of her early retirement.

The man is utterly immoral: he has no *principles* whatsoever.

Remember, if it doesn't make you too uncomfortable, "The princi*pal* is your *pal*." That's the way to spell the school head and *everything else except the rule*—and *rule* and *principle* both end in silent *e*.

The adjective, meaning chief, main, most important, is also *principal*.

My *principal* concern regarding the trip is my daughter's safety.

✻

select   extra nice; choice

selected   chosen; picked out; some, not others

The distinction has been blurred somewhat by Madison Avenue; pay no heed.

A *select* quartet of dancers will perform for His Royal Highness.

Selected items will go on sale at midnight.

✻

electrocute (ih·LEK·truh·kyute') To kill with electricity: by lightning, electrical current, or the electric chair. The word is a made-up combination of the prefix *electr-* and *-cute*, as in *execute*. Although death by electricity has been around forever, the word was not coined until 1889, with the advent of the electric chair.

serve   to wait on like a servant; to care for someone's needs

service   to fix or maintain, as a vehicle; on a farm, to have sexual relations with

It's our pleasure to *serve* any member of the Duchess's household!

The man who *services* my car has a PhD in anthropology.

Please do not say *service* when you simply mean *serve*. Look at that definition! Unless you are talking about breeding livestock or keeping your pickup truck in good running order, the word is *serve*. Oh—banks like to talk about *servicing* loans, and that's okay.

✳

their   belonging to those people or things

there   not here, but in that location; used in the idioms *there is* and *there are* as well

they're   contraction of *they are*

  They stored *their* furniture and cruised the Mediterranean for three years.

  There were 90 sailors who needed overnight lodgings there in that tiny village.

  They're such social climbers Lois won't even invite them over for a drink.

These three words are homonyms, which sound just alike but have different meanings. Chapter 6 lists a number of them for you. You should know that, in most cases, spellcheckers won't warn you if you're using the wrong homonym. Watch this: Their not able to tell the difference. There not able to tell the difference. My spelling and grammar checker had no problem with those two incorrect substitutes for *they're*. You're on your own: scary stuff.

WordSet II: In Visceral, Excruciating Pain, Debra Has Paramount Need for Help

Debra didn't see the tree root on the biking trail **eroded** by the spring rains. She swerved too late. The dirt bike went airborne, seemed to **hover** impossibly, then landed heavily.

SHE CURSED HER **AUDACITY**

THE PAIN WAS **EXCRUCIATING**

The pain that coursed through her left foot was **excruciating**. **Gingerly** she lifted the bike and, bending her knee, **contrived** to free her left leg. She took off her helmet and her motocross gloves—the left one was shredded but **providentially** her hand was unhurt—and began to **assess** her situation.

She wasn't hurt, apparently, except for her foot, now swelling rapidly and turning an **ominous** blue. Her ankle felt badly sprained. Possibly something might be broken: She couldn't put weight on it or move it properly. ICE: ice, compress, elevate. She needed to treat it before the pain got worse.

She looked at her bike. The front tire was flat and the **chassis** was bent at an improbable angle. She wasn't leaving the woods on that. She opened her backpack to **extricate** her cell phone. "No Service," **proclaimed** the screen. That wasn't good. Jake knew she was biking in Dane Barth State Forest, but the area **boasted** miles and miles of trails; she'd be tough to find. The day was hot and **sultry**; she batted at buzzing flies with a **futile** effort.

She hesitated briefly, then tore off three long strips from her shirt and bound them around her ankle. She propped her foot at a **jaunty** angle on the bike seat. Applying the cold pack from her lunch to the ankle, she then swallowed three pain pills with some Gatorade and a few bites of her sandwich. Just minutes ago she'd been **ravenous**, but the pain had taken her appetite.

Getting help was **paramount**. Or getting *to* help. In **retrospect**, biking alone in an area **notorious** for lack of cell tower coverage hadn't been smart. She cursed her **audacity**. She shouted "Help!" loudly but not hopefully: Dane Barth was so **vast** that it was unlikely another person was in close **proximity** or even anywhere for miles. Jake was, **inopportunely**, at a bike rally near Petersburg until late that night. No one else knew her whereabouts. A check of her trail map **verified** that she was at least 6 miles from the nearest staffed cabin. With a branch for support, could she hop or hobble to civilization? She had a **visceral** feeling it wouldn't work. The pain in her ankle was so bad that the slightest motion **elicited** tears.

Suddenly she heard the roar of a four-stroke engine as a ranger helicopter flew overhead. **Elated**, she waved her sweater rapidly back and forth. Her joy was **ephemeral**: The copter kept going. She realized that attracting attention would greatly **enhance** her chances of rescue.

A fire! Fires were **proscribed** in Dane Barth. Smoke would bring someone to investigate. With so much rain recently, she didn't fear a forest fire. She **rummaged** in her tool kit and found a pack of matches. She got crumpled paper from her backpack, some dry twigs, a little 3-in-One Oil, and a couple of branches from the trail's edge: She was in business! She poured Gatorade on her merrily burning fire and was rewarded by an **imposing** plume of smoke. As if by magic, the chopper reappeared. Again she waved frantically. This time the helicopter dipped a salute, then landed in a nearby clearing. The rangers stowed the bike and lifted Debra carefully aboard. Borne to safety, she felt her pain **evaporate** in an **abundance** of gratitude.

Debra's Words, 1st Third

eroded (ee·ROE·ded) To erode is to destroy or wear away—as by the activity of water, or wind, or even a glacier. Erosion can take a long time. For example, a cave may be made by centuries of waves breaking against a rock cliff. George's drinking problem *eroded* our friendship. In this story, erosion hasn't taken place over time: Roots are sticking out of the ground because recent rain has worn away the dirt on the path.

hover (HUH·ver) To hang in the air. Hummingbirds *hover*, wings whirring, and that's the sense in which the word's used here. Hover also means to move back and forth but always nearby—like a *hover* mother, for instance, too protective to leave her child, or like a fever that *hovers* near 102 degrees.

excruciating (ex·KROO·shee·ate´·ing) Intensely painful; almost unbearable. The word is derived from the same Latin root as crucify. Whatever Debra's done, it really hurts. Except for agonizing, I don't know any synonyms. A useful word.

gingerly (JIN·jer·lee) Very cautiously and carefully, perhaps with feelings of reluctance or fear. I stepped *gingerly* out onto the tiny porch high above the city. He lifted the dangerous insect *gingerly* with gloved hands. If you're uncertain what the outcome will be, your activity is probably going to be gingerly. The word is an adjective also, meaning cautious or wary: A painting conservator approaches an old painting in a *gingerly* fashion.

contrived (kun·TRIVED) As a verb, to manage or devise; to come up with, as a plan. We *contrived* a meeting between Fay and Nick. Contrived can also mean too intricate, or overdone, maybe even faked: The touching scene between June and her daughter looked *contrived* to me. One dictionary says "not spontaneous." Exactly.

providentially (proh´·vih·DEN·shuh·lee) Luckily; fortunately. As if guided by providence, providence being a synonym for God or fate. The word suggests that whichever one you are referencing is in a good mood. I was 20 minutes late for the train; *providentially*, the train was 30 minutes late. The adjective is providential: Our meeting is *providential*, as I've been wanting to ask you for a loan. (In this case one must ask, providential for whom?)

assess (uh·SESS) To find out or determine the extent, value, or amount of something. If I'm assessing your property for tax purposes, I'm trying to figure out how valuable it is. You can also assess damage, or assess a problem, as Debra is doing here. Assessing is getting your arms around the situation.

ominous (AH·min·uss) Indicating that some evil or catastrophic thing is about to happen; foreboding. We heard the *ominous* roll of thunder and realized a storm was coming. An *ominous* black cloud blocked the sun. The soldier's appearance at our door seemed *ominous*. An omen is a sign, which may be good or bad. Ominous tends to be only bad.

chassis (CHA·see, SHA·see) The word comes from the French *chaise*, which means chair. A chassis is a supporting frame of a structure: A computer or a TV set has a chassis. People often speak of the chassis of a car, which may include such "running gear" as the engine and driveshaft. The frame of Debra's motor bike is all bent out of shape from her accident.

extricate (EX·trih·kate´) To rid oneself or another of an entanglement or problem; to get someone or something out of a difficult situation. I realized Mrs. Wales wanted me to chair the committee, and I struggled to *extricate* myself from her clutches. The suggestion is that Debra has to fish around in the backpack before she can wrest her phone from the bottom of the bag.

proclaimed (proe·KLAMED) To proclaim means to declare to the world, usually with pride. The king *proclaimed* the joyful news that he and the queen had a daughter. The newspaper headline *proclaimed* the end of the war. The word is used ironically here: What the phone is proclaiming is not good news to Debra. The noun is proclamation: The town issued a *proclamation* honoring the oldest living inhabitant.

✹ PRACTICING DEBRA'S WORDS, 1ST THIRD

The words for the first third of Debra's story are:

assess	excruciating	hover
chassis	extricate	ominous
contrived	gingerly	proclaimed
eroded		providentially

A. Fill in the blanks with the correct list words.

1. John's bad behavior _____ my confidence in him.

2. I walked _____ around the spiny sea urchins littering the beach.

3. Although she tried not to _____, Bettina was overly protective of her daughter.

4. My embarrassment was _____ when I couldn't remember my cousin's name.

B. If your truck's chassis needs work, the shop will be working on the _____.

1. seats   3. engine

2. cab   4. frame and running gear

C. Lost is to haphazardly as saved is to _____.

D. Which list word is the closest antonym for *insert*?

E. Match the list words with their correct definitions in the right-hand column.

1. contrived   a. publicized proudly

2. ominous   b. estimate

3. assess   c. overdone, artificial

4. proclaimed   d. foreboding

F. Complete the following story with list words.

While the mechanic examined my car's (frame) to (determine the extent of) the damage, I could only (hang closely around), suffering (agonizing) pangs of anxiety, and occasionally (cautiously) venturing a question, which he didn't answer. His silence seemed (threatening, boding ill) to me. Suddenly he turned and (announced), "Not too bad! (Fortunately), you (managed) not to hit the wall straight on, so your suspension is undamaged. We can probably (remove, free) you from this mess for very little money."

Answers

A. 1. eroded; 2. gingerly; 3. hover; 4. excruciating

B. 4

C. providentially

D. extricate

E. 1. c; 2. d; 3. b; 4. a

F. chassis; assess; hover; excruciating; gingerly; ominous; proclaimed; Providentially; contrived; extricate

Debra's Words, 2nd Third

boasted (BOE·sted) The verb boast means, for one thing, to brag; to talk big. Whereas proclaim means to speak or write with pride, boast is over the top: If you boast, you're too pleased with yourself. But the word may also be used, as it is here, in a positive sense: If we say the reservation boasts miles of trails, that simply means it has or possesses many trails, which it can call attention to with (pardonable) pride. New England *boasts* many historic houses.

sultry (SUL·tree) Humid and hot. Tropical weather is often sultry, and August often has many sultry days. Someone or something that can excite sexual desire may also be termed sultry: On a *sultry* evening, that *sultry* damsel was sending *sultry* looks my way.

futile (FYOO·tull, FYOO·tile) Useless; ineffective. Debra's getting nowhere chasing away those flies. The word is often paired, as it is here, with effort(s): His efforts to make conversation were *futile*. The opposite of futile, interestingly, is utile, which rhymes.

jaunty (JAWN·tee) Lively; or spirited in looks or behavior; sporty. Debra has stuck her foot up on the bike seat so it looks kind of cute; this suggests she hasn't lost her spirit. Joan wore a *jaunty* beret tipped over one eye. The man about town sported a *jaunty* silk ascot at his neck.

ravenous (RA·veh·nuss) That's *ra* as in *rap*. Extremely hungry, greedy; having a huge appetite. By extension, the word means hungry not only for food: You can be ravenous for power, or fame, or even a good bottle of wine. A close synonym is *voracious*. Both mean characterized by limitless greed.

paramount (PA·ruh·mount´) And that's *pa* as in *pack*. Supreme; chief or dominant; of overriding importance. The most important thing to Debra right now is to get assistance. The word comes from Latin, meaning "above the mountain." I might tell my staff it's paramount to get the direct-mail piece out to the entire customer base as the new product launches. I can also say it's of paramount importance.

retrospect (REH·truh·spekt´) A review of the past or an event in the past. We use the word overwhelmingly in the phrase "in retrospect," meaning in looking back over an event or the past. In *retrospect*, riding your bike with no hands isn't such a good idea, said Jane from her hospital bed. Hindsight is 20-20, as they say, and Debra realizes in *retrospect*, or hindsight, that she's done something not too smart.

notorious (noe·TORE·ee·us) From the root word for knowledge, the word means well known in a negative sense. My sister was *notorious* for forgetting where she'd parked her car. Our post office is *notorious* for delivering mail several days late. Everyone knows it. Just as everyone knows that the part of the reservation Debra has been riding in doesn't have good cell phone coverage.

audacity (aw·DA·sih·tee) Boldness, nerve, confidence, lack of fear. If you're audacious, you're the opposite of timid or frightened—sometimes a little too lacking in fear. Someone with audacity has crossed a line and is almost arrogant with self-confidence. Debra's knocking herself for having had the *audacity* to think nothing bad was going to happen to her.

vast (VAST: rhymes with *past*) Huge; enormous; wide-reaching. He had a *vast* store of knowledge about insects that he loved to share. A desert is often called vast; so is Antarctica. The adverb vastly means enormously or extensively: She is *vastly* competent, able to do a thousand things well and usually at once. The noun is vastness: The *vastness* of the empty theater gave me the creeps.

✸PRACTICING DEBRA'S WORDS, 2ND THIRD

The words for the second third of Debra's story are:

audacity	jaunty	retrospect
boasted	notorious	sultry
futile	paramount	vast
	ravenous	

A. Which word is the closest synonym for *boasted*?
1. attempted
2. bragged
3. haggled
4. cooked

B. Fill in the blanks with the correct list words.

1. Betsy was _____ for borrowing things and not returning them.

2. I discovered there is a _____ area of the United States that is flat as a board.

3. After three days in the elevator, Ronald was _____.

4. Jane is so sensitive that not hurting Rachel's feelings is _____ with her.

C. Choose the correct definition for the following list words.

1. audacity
   a. boldness
   b. calm, serenity
   c. high spirits, joy
   d. fame

2. sultry
   a. gloomy
   b. sullen, pouting
   c. sexy, hot
   d. huge, wide

3. retrospect
   a. close inspection
   b. hindsight
   c. telescope
   d. past

4. jaunty
   a. yellowish, gold
   b. lively
   c. grotesque
   d. painful

D. Which sentence uses the word *futile* correctly?

1. Your hat is perfect with your magenta outfit; what a futile choice!

2. Thank you for your futile offer to drive us to Carmel: We accept with pleasure.

3. It's futile to beg your father to go, as he's made up his mind to stay home.

4. As a result of his long career, everyone knew the futile outlaw's face.

E. Complete the following story with list words:

His hat at a (perky) angle over one eye, Jonah (talked big) about his lady friends. His ways with women were (famous, in a negative sense): his (boldness) and (greedy) appetite had led to (enormous) numbers of conquests. His (useless) attempts to enchant the (sexy) Renata, however, had frustrated him. In (looking to the past), she may have been the only one to refuse him, making her of (supreme) importance in his mind.

Answers

A. 2

B. 1. notorious; 2.vast; 3. ravenous; 4. paramount

C. 1. a; 2. c; 3. b; 4. b

D. 3

E. jaunty; boasted; notorious; audacity; ravenous; vast, futile; sultry; retrospect; paramount

---

Please Don't Say That!
in parentheses (in pah·REN·thih·seez) Enclosed by parentheses. Some people pronounce this familiar phrase as if it were "in parenthesis." A parenthesis is one of those little bracketing gizmos: ( ), and they come in pairs. It is a physical impossibility to put anything in parenthes*is*, because you'd have only one of them. So be sure, if you're using the phrase in conversation, to pronounce that last syllable *seez*.

Debra's Words, 3rd Third

proximity (prok·SIM·ih·tee) Nearness or closeness. The *proximity* of the house to an excellent public school added greatly to its value. His *proximity* to his despised stepbrother made him feel ill. "It was unlikely another person was in close proximity" to Debra is a fairly stuffy way to say nobody was likely to be anywhere near her, but I wanted to use the word.

inopportunely (in·ah´·pore·TOON·lee, in·ah´·pore·TYUNE·lee) Inconveniently; at the just-wrong moment. My company arrived early and *inopportunely*: Dressed only in my bathrobe, I was taking out the trash. Jake's trip is *inopportune* because he's not around to worry about where Debra is.

verified (VEH·rih·fide´) To verify means to confirm; to establish the truth, accuracy, or reality of something. The jeweler *verified* that my watch was 14-carat gold. The airline representative *verified* the plane's scheduled departure. Using her map, Debra verifies that she is indeed miles from help.

visceral (VISS·uh·rull) Your viscera are your vital organs, such as your heart, lungs, and liver. (The singular, for your information, is viscus.) Therefore, anything felt in a visceral way is felt at a very deep, instinctive level, as opposed to an intellectual level. Debra has an intuitive feeling she won't be able to cover 6 miles with her injured leg. You might have a visceral dislike for someone: You haven't got evidence the person's a baddie; you just feel it, as it were, in your gut.

elicited (ee·LIH·sih·ted) To elicit means to bring out or draw forth, usually a response. If I elicit information from you, I draw it out of you; to elicit sympathy is to bring it out in your hearers; if I elicit a round of applause, I've called it forth from my audience. Debra's pain is such that simply moving elicits tears. Don't confuse this word with *illicit*, which means illegal or forbidden.

elated (ee·LAY·ted) Filled with high spirits; overjoyed; exultant. To elate means to fill with pride or joy. I was *elated* to learn I was a finalist for the prize. *Elated* by the success of the fund-raising dinner, she called for a toast. Debra is elated to see the helicopter that can carry her to safety.

ephemeral (eh·FEM·eh·rull) From the Greek *ephemeros*, lasting one day only, ephemeral means lasting just a short time. The life span of a mayfly is *ephemeral*: It lives, depending on the species, a few hours or a few days. Debra's delight upon seeing the helicopter is fleeting; it goes by without noticing her.

enhance (en·HANCE) To enhance means to add to in a positive way, to improve something in quality or value. Joan's friendship has *enhanced* Rita's stay in Portland. The new rug *enhances* the charm of the dining room. Debra's chances for rescue will be enhanced if she can attract the attention of a helicopter pilot or other reservation staff.

proscribed (proe·SKRIBED) Forbidden or prohibited. If I proscribe entrance into my yard, I prohibit anyone from coming in. Aiding a criminal is *proscribed* by law. Because fires are proscribed in Dane Barth, Debra realizes she'll be noticed by the authorities if she starts one. Proscribe is spelled very much like *prescribe*, but the two words have very different meanings: Prescribe means to give as a rule or guide, or to issue a medical prescription. Dr. Mason *prescribed* two weeks at the seashore to cure my insomnia.

rummage (RUM·ij) To make a thorough search by rooting around and disarranging the contents of whatever you're searching in. If you rummage, you aren't sure where what you're looking for may be, and chances are good you make a mess by your rummaging. Rummage, as you probably know, is "a confusion of miscellaneous articles," as one dictionary puts it, or a bunch of stuff. At a *rummage* sale, you can *rummage* through other people's stuff.

imposing (im·POE·zing) Impressive; striking; grand because of size or dignity. The façade of the new building is *imposing*, built of marble and cherry wood, and embellished with gold leaf. (To embellish means to decorate so as to beautify.) At 6 feet and with the manners of an empress, Mrs. Sargent cuts an *imposing* figure. To Debra's delight, the liquid she pours on her fire generates an imposing—a big and impressive—column of smoke.

evaporate (ee·VAP·uh·rate´) From the same root word as vapor, this verb means to turn into vapor or steam, as fog evaporates when the sun comes up. By extension, it can mean to disappear: My anger *evaporated* when I saw how sorry he was. Debra's pain vanishes as she realizes she's safe.

abundance (a·BUN·dunce) Plentiful quantity, at least sufficient and maybe more than enough. If I have an abundance of wealth, I have lots and lots of money. The forest had an *abundance* of game: It *abounded* with game. To abound and abundance are from the same Latin word, which means to overflow. Debra is overflowing with gratitude.

✺ PRACTICING DEBRA'S WORDS, 3RD THIRD

The words for the last third of Debra's story are:

abundance	ephemeral	proximity
elated	evaporate	rummage
elicited	imposing	verified
enhance	inopportunely	visceral
	proscribed	

A. Fill in the blanks with the correct list words.

　1. Her new father-in-law was _____: 6 feet 3 inches tall, with a profile like a hawk.

　2. My son's goals are _____: They come and go, depending on his moods.

　3. Please don't _____ through my purse—I wrote down some nasty remarks about you.

　4. You can make salt at the beach by simply letting ocean water _____ in the sun.

　5. Travel out of the country was _____ until Ronald McDonald was found.

B. Which list word is the closest antonym for *spoil*?

C. Which of the following words means *elated*?
1. bloated   3. delighted
2. silly   4. tardy

D. Match the list words with their correct definitions in the right-hand column.
1. elicited   a. nearness
2. proximity   b. made certain of the accuracy of
3. verified   c. deep, instinctive
4. visceral   d. at an inconvenient time
5. inopportunely   e. drew forth

E. Which list word is appropriate on Thanksgiving?

F. Complete the following story with list words:

Mary Sue's beauty was of the (temporary) kind, while her sister Jennifer (called forth) undying devotion with her timeless charm. (Nearness) to either one gave me a (deep, in the gut) feeling of happiness. I was (overjoyed) when Jennifer invited me to a party. But my boss (unfortunately, inconveniently) asked me to work that night; the party was (forbidden). My boss was (impressive), even scary. I was afraid to say no. My elation began to (vanish). Perhaps my unavailability would (add to) my charm in Jennifer's eyes, but I wasn't counting on it.

Answers

A. 1. imposing; 2. ephemeral; 3. rummage; 4. evaporate; 5. proscribed

B. enhance

C. 3

D. 1. e; 2. a; 3. b; 4. c; 5. d

E. abundance

F. ephemeral; elicited; proximity; visceral; elated; inopportunely; proscribed; imposing; evaporate; enhance

Oops! Words That Don't Mean What You Think

Some words mean something quite different from what, by their looks, their sound, or the way other people are using them, they *ought* to mean. Here are a few. Be warned! You never want to embarrass yourself by using a word incorrectly. Also note that just because a dictionary lists a meaning doesn't necessarily mean it's correct by most people's standards: Dictionaries are to some extent *descriptive* rather than *prescriptive*—that is, they sometimes describe what's going on in a language, whether it's correct or not. Case in point: You'll always find *ain't* in the dictionary, but you wouldn't dream of using it. I hope.

antebellum

If you took Latin, you know that *bellum* means war. So antebellum must mean antiwar, right? Sorry, no. The clue is that the prefix *anti-* means against, but the prefix *ante-* (that's an e) means before. This word accordingly means "before the war," usually referring to the American Civil War.

anxious

This word, as you probably know, means worried, concerned for the future. You may also think it means eager, as in "I'm anxious to see you." You should know that 53 percent of the *American Heritage Dictionary's* Usage Panel (2006) rejects this usage. Ta-da! If you're eager, say eager. Save anxious for your concerned and worried experiences.

chauvinist

A chauvinist is someone who is madly supportive of some person, place, or cause, and applies particularly to excessive patriotism. It has nothing necessarily to do with men who put down women—although the term *male chauvinist pig* caught on in the 1960s to describe someone, often in a position of authority, who believes men are superior to women and doesn't hesitate to speak and act on that premise.

decimate

Today the primary meaning of decimate is to reduce catastrophically: Infectious disease has decimated the population of deer in this region. You should know, however, that the verb originally meant to kill or take away 10 percent, or one in 10, which is unfortunate rather than catastrophic. It's possible you could run into a stickler who'd object to your using decimate to mean devastate, so I'm giving you a heads up.

disinterested

I can't blame you if you think this word means lacking interest. Some people use it that way, and most dictionaries accept that meaning. In fact, disinterested and its relative, *un*interested, have exchanged meanings over several centuries. But disinterested has the very interesting meaning of impartial, evenhanded—the way justice is supposed to be. Many well-informed and well-educated people prefer to use it in that way. Why not? And use uninterested to mean not interested. Works for me.

fulsome

This word looks as though it should mean full or abundant, and it can indeed mean that. But those well-informed people get into the act again and point out that fulsome can mean fawning, or revoltingly insincere—heaping on abundant praise, for example, but hypocritically. This meaning is enough to keep me from ever, ever using it in its "good" sense.

infamous

It ought to mean not famous, right? Or very famous. It doesn't. In fact, it means notorious, or famous for something bad. Everyone remembers John's infamous practical joke, which resulted in Aunt Mary's broken leg. A criminal is infamous, as is a crime. Mussolini and Hitler were infamous, as were their respective ideologies, Fascism and Nazism.

inflammable

If flammable means capable of catching fire, then inflammable must mean *in*capable of catching fire, right? Wrong. Inflammable means capable of catching fire. I told you English isn't fair. The opposite of flammable is flameproof. The *American Heritage Dictionary of the English Language* suggests never using *inflammable* on product labels, as some buyers might be misled. Indeed.

invaluable

Same idea. Valuable means prized, so invaluable ought to mean not prized. But it means priceless, of value so great it can't be estimated. Good grief. Be thankful if English is your native tongue: Imagine how hard it would be to learn a language as tricky as this one.

noisome

Sounds like a good party—maybe a too-good party, complete with complaining neighbors—but this word actually means harmful, toxic, or repulsive to the senses, especially the sense of smell. Paint fumes may be noisome, or a noisome odor may be coming from the swamp out back.

nonplussed

Some people must have this word confused with nonchalant, which means not flustered. At any rate, a lot of people think it means that. In fact, nonplussed means taken aback, confused, bemused, all that not-on-top-of-it stuff. If I'm nonplussed by your comment, I don't know what to make of it.

penultimate

A friend of mine had a boss who was sure that penultimate meant THE ultimate, the absolute greatest. If you thought so too, repent. It simply means the next-to-last: I knew I could count on you to grab the penultimate cookie. Here comes the Latin again: *Paene* means *almost*, *ultima* means *last*. The word peninsula comes from this same *paene* and the Latin word for island, *insula*. A peninsula is a body of land almost, but not quite, surrounded by water—almost an island.

plausible

This word is one to watch out for. Although it has a primary meaning of credible or believable, it also means giving a *deceptive* impression of truth or believability. A plausible explanation is one that may not, in fact, be true. As I said, watch out.

5

WordSet III: Jim's Lingering on the Verge of a Subconscious Disinclination

As Jim raced up the stairs to the office, he wondered for the thousandth time why he was always on the **verge** of being late. It wasn't because he stayed in bed too long. He set the alarm clock to give him *three hours* to shower, shave, dress, eat breakfast, and **traverse** the city, a 45-minute commute, to get to the office. And it wasn't a **disinclination** to go to work, either; he actually liked his job as a graphic designer for a good-sized Web design firm. He thought once more that he was probably **lingering** too long over his morning newspaper—the crossword and the Sudoku in particular. Or that his **subconscious** mind got a **perverse** thrill out of sprinting in just under the wire. He sighed. He'd made it: only one minute late. But he couldn't keep on this way. He had some ideas; they just needed to **jell** a bit more.

ATTIRED IN JEANS AND A SWEATSHIRT, HER HAIR IN A DISHEVELED PONYTAIL, SHE LOOKED YOUNG AND DEFENSELESS

As he settled down at his desk, he **observed** a small envelope taped to the back of his monitor so just a corner showed. Opening it, he was **bemused** to discover a note from the administrative assistant he shared with several others. *Can you meet me on the fire escape at 10?* it read. *I need to speak to you. It's **crucial***. The note was signed *Vivian*. She lived near him. They had met on the train together a couple of times when his car was in the shop. He didn't know her that well—he was aware she was pleasant and **competent** and anything but **indolent**, but that was about it—and was astonished that she should make him her **confidant**.

At 10 o'clock, Jim stepped out onto the fire escape, where smokers often took their breaks. Vivian had **preceded** him. **Attired** in jeans and a pink sweatshirt, her light brown hair in a **disheveled** ponytail, she looked young and defenseless. And, at the moment, **disconsolate**: Her eyes were cast down and her shoulders slumped.

"Thank you for meeting me," she said. "I feel terrible bothering you, but I don't know what to do. Nick's been e-mailing me a lot of **inappropriate** messages. He says he wants to see me, I'm beautiful, he can't concentrate, that kind of thing. I keep telling him no, I don't respond to the e-mails, I try to ignore him. I can't stand him." She made a **dismissive** gesture.

Nick was their **immediate** boss, and a married man. Jim didn't like him much, but they had a comfortable working relationship.

"I know I have all kinds of **recourse**," Vivian continued. "I can file a complaint with human resources, I can have him **disciplined**, but he'll make my life miserable if I do. And if I leave, he's not going to write me a recommendation, and if I try to explain, no one's ever going to want to hire me—they'll think I did something to deserve the **harassment**. Or they'll think I'm a trouble-maker."

It was true, Jim realized. He thought about her **predicament** and was filled with **compassion**. He was sure Vivian hadn't asked for this. And he felt a **simmering** rage at the system that would allow her to be treated badly and then punished for it. Despite all the strides women have made, this sort of thing still happened. He wasn't a bleeding-heart woman's libber, but this was **egregiously** unfair.

"I've been on the Internet looking for another job," Vivian said, "But with the state of the economy, there's not much out there."

"Don't do anything for now," he told her. "Keep on refusing him. Don't get angry—just play it cool. I may have a solution to your **dilemma**."

He went back to his desk and worked steadily for several hours. After lunch, he did some work of his own. The next day, he did some **calculations** and called his bank. Early the next week, he approached Vivian's desk.

"How would you like to join a very small firm with outstanding growth **potential**?" he asked her. "I'm going out on my own, Vivian. Will you come to work for me?"

Her face broke into smiles. "You're starting your own company so I'll have a place to work?" she asked **incredulously**.

"I've been thinking about it for quite a while," he **acknowledged**. "Your predicament just **impelled** me to get going."

"I'll get out of here!" Vivian exulted.

"And I'll never be late again," said Jim.

Jim's Words, 1st Third

verge (VERJ) Edge or threshold. Almost always used with "on the" to mean almost there. If you're on the verge of discovering a cure for the common cold, you're going to be famous very soon. Jane is on the *verge* of marrying that horrible Hector!

traverse (truh·VURSS, TRA·vurss) To travel or pass across; to cross. Jim has to go through the city to get to his job.

Amazingly, *dictionary.com* gives 29 definitions for this word. It's a noun, a verb, and an adjective, and figures in sailing, skiing, surveying, and shooting! Look it up and enjoy.

disinclination (diss·in´·klih·NAY·shun) Unwillingness; foot-dragging; dislike; the condition of not wanting to do something. His adolescence was marked by a strong *disinclination* for work. The verb is to disincline: If I'm disinclined to share an apartment, I don't feel like doing it.

lingering (LING·gurr·ing) The verb to linger means to stay longer than necessary or expected, as if not wanting to leave: We *lingered* at the party and were among the last to leave. It can also mean to dawdle, or kill time, or move slowly. And it can mean to persist or remain alive, though feeble: The song's over, but the melody *lingers* on. He *lingered* in a coma for months after the accident.

subconscious (sub´·KON·shuss) In the mind although not available on a conscious level: Your subconscious thoughts may be rebellious, for example, while on the surface you are feeling and behaving cooperatively. Subconscious is also a noun: My *subconscious* is begging me to eat Hostess Twinkies.

perverse (purr·VURSS) Contrary; obstinate; cranky; persistent even when wrong; not what's expected or desired; sometimes not in one's best interests. When I heard Sam explaining the theory of black holes, I had a *perverse* urge to tell him to shut up. It's also a synonym for perverted, meaning twisted or turned away from what's right or good.

jell (JELL) To take shape; to solidify in a figurative or literal sense. You may wish to let the results of a meeting jell with your colleagues over the weekend. Jim's ideas need to become more coherent. This is, of course, the word from which we get the universal sick person's food, Jell-O.

observed (obb·ZURVD) The verb to observe means to notice; to see. If you observe something, you register it on your radar screen. The word is also a synonym for *said*, in the sense of "saw and commented on it": "Your son's hair is just like his father's," Madison *observed*. We tend to think observing is judgment-free: an impartial *observer*.

bemused (bee·MEWZD) (The verb is to bemuse.) Lost in thought; confused; astonished; maybe a little bewildered. Jim wasn't expecting this note. I was *bemused* by Angela's friendly behavior: I was pretty sure she disliked me. Sometimes the bemusement comes with a little chuckle attached. What's this? Who, me?

crucial (KROO·shul) Critically important; a decisive factor. Vivian's trying to tell him she's not just fooling around—this is a matter of great concern. Like other strong adjectives, *crucial* shouldn't be modified, or further described. Don't say *very crucial*, just as I hope you wouldn't say *very desperate*. Such adjectives stand on their own: Either something is crucial or it isn't.

competent (KOMM·puh·tuhnt) Able; capable; qualified because of possessing the necessary skills. If you're good at what you're doing, you're competent. *Incompetent* is the opposite. You can also use it in a way that isn't so complimentary: It can mean adequate, good but perhaps lacking inspiration: a *competent* performance of Beethoven's Seventh Symphony.

✹ PRACTICING JIM'S WORDS, 1ST THIRD

The words for the first third of Jim's story are:

bemused	jell	perverse
competent	lingering	subconscious
crucial	observed	traverse
disinclination		verge

A. Which list word is the closest synonym for *reluctance*?

B. Fill in the blanks with the correct list words.

　　1. The actors have learned their lines and gestures, but the production still has to _____.

　　2. It's _____ that you bring the tickets; otherwise we'll have to pay twice.

　　3. You're so accident prone, I wonder whether your _____ is trying to punish you.

　　4. He's on the _____ of a great medical breakthrough, so don't bother him!

　　5. I tried to _____ the icy hill on my new skis, with disastrous results.

C. Which list word are you likely to use when writing about bird-watching?

D. Match the list words with their correct definitions in the right-hand column.

　　1. bemused　　　　　a. capable

　　2. competent　　　　b. cranky, contrary

　　3. lingering　　　　c. staying on, dawdling

　　4. perverse　　　　d. bewildered

E. Complete the following story with list words.

　　Mary is a (handy, able) young woman with a (critical) flaw: a serious (unwillingness) to get and keep a job. I'm (puzzled, confused) by this odd trait, which I've (noticed) for some time. Perhaps it's a (persisting) desire to stay a child, or a (wrong-headed) need to fail coming from her (not available in the conscious) mind. Whatever it is, she's on the (brink) of losing yet another situation. I gave her some advice but it didn't (take shape) in her mind. If she's going to (move along in) this life successfully, she needs to shape up.

Answers

A. disinclination

B. 1. jell; 2. crucial; 3. subconscious; 4. verge; 5. traverse

C. observed

D. 1. d; 2. a; 3. c; 4. b

E. competent; crucial; disinclination; bemused; observed; lingering; perverse; subconscious; verge; jell; traverse

MacGuffin (muh·GUH·fin) This word can be useful when you're talking about movies, books, or plays. A MacGuffin is the item around which a plot revolves: The necklace that the burglars stole, for example, causes the burglars to run, the detectives to pursue. In a spy movie, it's usually the papers—it doesn't really matter *what* papers, but someone has them and someone else is desperate to get them. The key in *Pirates of the Caribbean: Dead Man's Chest* is the MacGuffin. The item may itself be trivial, but it gets the action going.

Jim's Words, 2nd Third

indolent (IN·duh·luhnt) Habitually lazy; sluggish; unwilling to stir. I picture a Southern belle lying on a chaise, languidly fanning herself. Marcia is *indolent* unless she thinks somebody's watching. If Jim characterizes Vivian as not indolent, he's saying she's energetic, proactive—all that good stuff you want in your employees.

confidant (KONN·fih·DAHNT, KONN·fih·DANT) From the French; somebody whom you trust enough to confide your secrets and private matters to. Henry was his only *confidant*; he told no one else. The word can apply to either men or women, but there's also a word *confidante*, used for a woman only. Don't confuse either word with *confident*, which means certain, secure, sure of oneself.

preceded (pree·SEE·dehd) To precede means to come before, in time, in space, or in a figurative sense. *A* words *precede B* words in the dictionary, and Vivian has preceded Jim by arriving first. We get a fabulous noun from the same root and prefix: *precedent* (PREH·suh·dent), which means something done earlier that establishes an example or mode of procedure for future behavior: Lawyers typically base cases on *precedent*.

attired (at·TIRED) The verb is to attire or to be attired. Dressed; clothed in. Attired goes nicely with gorgeous clothing—the queen was *attired* in ermine and purple velvet—though it works fine for jeans as well. Attire is the noun: You should wear formal *attire* to the coronation or you won't be invited again.

disheveled (dih·SHEV·uhld) Messed up; in disorder or disarray. Vivian's disheveled ponytail, accordingly, is perhaps briefly combed and hastily pulled together. It doesn't look great. People who sleep in their clothes typically find their clothes are *disheveled* when they wake up. They themselves will also look *disheveled*. The verb is to dishevel: The wind *disheveled* my hair.

disconsolate (diss·KONN·suh·luht) Unhappy; sad; sorrowful; unable to be comforted. From the same root as console: If I'm disconsolate, you're not going to be able to console, or comfort, me. With her downcast eyes and slumping shoulders, Vivian is the picture of disconsolation.

inappropriate (in·app·PROE·pree·it) Not suitable; unseemly; not right for the situation. High-heeled shoes are *inappropriate* for a beach picnic, and hitting on a subordinate at work is deeply inappropriate.

dismissive (diss·MISS·ivv) Not seriously considering; rejecting. Vivian's gesture means she wouldn't dream of taking Nick up on his suggestions. Your reaction to my idea is so *dismissive* I'm sure you think it's a bad one. The verb dismiss can also mean to fire or to send away: The king *dismissed* the ambassadors.

immediate (im·MEE·dee·it) You know this word. It means prompt, done right away. But it can also mean right next to, without interruption: After the sign, take your *immediate* right, or, as in this case, Nick is Vivian and Jim's immediate boss, the very next person up the chain.

recourse (REE·KORSS, rih·KORSS) Access to someone or something for protection or assistance; a source of help. If you have no recourse, you have nowhere to turn. The word comes from the Latin *recurrere*, to run back. Vivian comments that she does have recourse, but every avenue has serious drawbacks.

disciplined (DISS·ih·plinnd) The verb to discipline means to punish, control, or correct. We *disciplined* the puppy by tapping him on the nose with a rolled-up newspaper when he misbehaved. It may take more than the newspaper to retrain Nick. Disciplined can also mean well organized in one's habits and performance, well trained, and controlled: To be a good rower, you must be *disciplined* as well as strong.

✳ PRACTICING JIM'S WORDS, 2ND THIRD

The words for the second third of Jim's story are:

attired	disheveled	inappropriate
confidant	dismissive	indolent
disciplined	immediate	preceded
disconsolate		recourse

A. Fill in the blanks with the correct list words.

1. Peggy was so rude and disorderly in class that I had no _____ but to send her to the principal.

2. My _____ son just lies in bed till 1:00 in the afternoon and won't even try to get a job.

3. Janet rushed in completely _____, her hair wild, her clothing a mess, screaming that the house was on fire.

4. The man who was sitting on my _____ left is a very eligible bachelor.

5. His fame _____ him: When he got to town, we already knew who he was.

B. You'd be _____ if, in an unguarded moment, you had told your deepest secret to your confidant.

　1. confused　　　　　　3. comfortable

　2. humiliated　　　　　　4. angry with yourself

C. Which sentence uses the word *inappropriate* correctly?

　1. Rover seems an inappropriate name for a dog.

　2. Susan's house sits out on an inappropriate point of land.

　3. My summer outfit was entirely inappropriate for the Winter Carnival.

　4. The inappropriate golf tournament hosted a number of pros.

D. Match the list words with their correct definitions in the right-hand column.

　1. attired　　　　　　a. rejecting

　2. disciplined　　　　b. controlled

　3. disconsolate　　　c. dressed

　4. dismissive　　　　d. despairing

E. Complete the following story with list words.

Mark was still (dressed) in his pajamas, his hair (in disorder), his expression (unhappy). I thought this was (unsuitable) on the morning that (came before) his wedding and, as his friend and (person one trusts), said so. It struck me that he was (lazy) and not very (organized). His (prompt) reaction was (not seriously considering [my statements]). I had no (choice, place to turn) but to hold his head under the shower.

Answers

A. 1. recourse; 2. indolent; 3. disheveled; 4. immediate;
    5. preceded
B. 2
C. 3
D. 1. c; 2. b; 3. d; 4. a
E. attired; disheveled; disconsolate; inappropriate;
    preceded; confidant; indolent; disciplined; immediate;
    dismissive; recourse

peccadillo (pekk·uh·DILL·o) A very small sin. This word comes to us directly from Spanish, in which *pecado* means sin. *Pecadillo* is the diminutive form, the form used to indicate that something is little; hence, a little sin. A sinlet, if you will.

Jim's Words, 3rd Third

harassment (huh·RASS·ment; the British say HARR·iss·ment) The act of annoying, bothering, or threatening someone with unwelcome or hostile attention. Sexual harassment is just one of many types of harassing behavior. A panhandler, for example, who aggressively pesters you for money is guilty of harassment.

predicament (pre·DICK·uh·mint) A situation, especially a problematic or difficult situation. I've lost my glasses and I didn't memorize my speech: I'm in a *predicament*. If you're in a predicament, the way out isn't immediately obvious.

compassion (kumm·PASH·un) Pity that has a strong awareness of another's pain, often mixed with a desire to help. Its Latin origins mean *with pain*—in other words, feeling someone else's misery.

simmering (SIMM·err·ing) The verb is to simmer. If water is simmering, it's just below boiling point. The word can be used either in fact or as if: If I'm simmering, I am experiencing inner turbulence—I could explode in anger or some other strong emotion. If a situation is simmering, it could break out in violence.

egregiously (ee·GREE·juss·lee) Outrageously; in a seriously awful manner; noticeably badly. Egregiously unfair, then, means *terribly* unfair. The word is used in a negative sense only: You don't say egregiously good.

dilemma (dih·LEMM·uh) A difficult choice between two alternatives—sometimes two unpleasant alternatives—or simply a problem that doesn't seem to have a reasonable solution. The word is increasingly used simply as a synonym for problem or predicament (see above in this set of words), though some grammarians frown on the usage.

calculations (cal´·cue·LAY·shuns) Mathematical totals; the process or the result of figuring out. According to my *calculations*, the North Pole should be right around here someplace. Calculation can also mean clever planning to advance one's own interests: A calculating person may be cunning and is definitely out for him- or herself.

potential (poe·TEN·shul) As a noun, as Jim is using it, this means possibility, the capability to develop and grow. Esther doesn't test well, but I believe she has the *potential* to develop into an excellent student. Potential is also an adjective that means possible, capable of developing into: Is Vivian a potential girlfriend for Jim?

incredulously (in·CRED·juh·luss·ly) In a disbelieving manner. The adjective is incredulous, meaning not believing. Vivian understandably can't believe Jim would start a company just to help her out, so she speaks incredulously.

acknowledged (ack·NOLL·ejd) The verb to acknowledge means to admit or agree, sometimes against one's wishes:

I *acknowledged* that my opponent had won the fight. It also means to recognize the existence or reality of: Stephen was forced to *acknowledge* the claims of his cousins.

impelled (im·PELLD) To impel is to force or push forward; to drive. Impelled and compelled share an element of meaning: You feel pressured to do something. When I saw the man beat his dog, I was *impelled* to stop him. Vivian's situation has driven Jim to take action.

✹ PRACTICING JIM'S WORDS, 3RD THIRD

The words for the last third of Jim's story are:

acknowledged	egregiously	incredulously
calculations	harassment	potential
compassion	impelled	predicament
dilemma		simmering

A. Fill in the blanks with the correct list words.

1. Benedict's _____ show that the company has been losing money steadily since 2005.

2. When he offered to take the baby on his motorcycle, Juliet stared at him _____.

3. The controversy over Aunt Bea's estate, _____ for months, threatens to erupt into full-scale family warfare.

4. If you think for one minute I'm coming with you, you're _____ mistaken.

B. Which two list words are close, if not exact, synonyms?

C. Match the list words with their correct definitions in the right-hand column.

1. acknowledged   a. pushed forward, driven
2. compassion   b. admitted, recognized
3. harassment   c. pity, sympathy
4. impelled   d. act of bothering or threatening

✳ 75

D. Which sentence uses the word *potential* correctly?

    1. She offered him a potential made of pomegranate juice, grenadine, and tonic.

    2. I'm in a bit of a financial potential since I lost my job last month.

    3. From Marcia's potential, Betsy has always had the best of everything.

    4. With her strong shoulders, Pam has the potential to be a competitive swimmer.

E. Complete the following story with list words.

What a (difficult choice)! Should I have (recognized) the (bad situation) my friend was in, or shown (sympathy) for her brother? He accused her of (very badly) mismanaging the family trusts, while she said his (threatening behavior) was ruining her life. According to my (results of figuring), taking sides had little (possibility) for success. Still, (driven) by a desire to help, I set up a meeting without telling each the other was coming, but he was (almost boiling) with anger from the moment he saw her, and she reacted (disbelievingly) to his very presence. Now my motto is Never Interfere in Another Family's Business.

Answers

A. 1. calculations; 2. incredulously; 3. simmering; 4. egregiously

B. dilemma, predicament

C. 1. b; 2. c; 3. d; 4. a

D. 4

E. dilemma; acknowledged; predicament; compassion; egregiously; harassment; calculations; potential; impelled; simmering; incredulously

6

Homonyms:
They're, Their, Don't Fret!

No, now that you mention it, that *isn't* the way to spell "there, there." Homonyms are words—such as *their*, *there*, and *they're*—that sound exactly alike, or very close to it, but have different meanings. The trick is to know how to spell the one you want. You almost certainly know the meaning of the following words, many of them simple ones, but do you choose the correct one in writing? Spelling a word incorrectly creates a terrible impression, so it's important to get it right. This section will help you distinguish between the word you want and its evil homonym!

Unfortunately, most computer spellcheckers can't tell the difference between homonyms and cheerfully agree that "Marcia *excepted* the invitation," for example, is good English. Run your eyes over this list and flag any that give you trouble. Take a look from time to time and when you're writing something important.

Note that this isn't a comprehensive list—I trust you to distinguish between to and two—but I have included some that may seem easy to you but that routinely trip up people like you who ought to know better.

accept   to welcome; to agree to

I plan to *accept* his invitation.

except   excluding; besides

Everyone was there *except* Kamila.

✳

ad short for advertisement

I saw your *ad* on *Monster.com*.

add to include; to increase

The sunshine *adds* to our enjoyment.

✳

affect, *v.* to have an effect on; to influence

The moon's cycle *affects* the tides.

affect, *v.* to put on; to pretend

He *affected* the manner of a Rockefeller.

effect, *v.* to bring about; to cause

These negotiations may *effect* a cease-fire.

affect, *n.* mood; show of emotion

The prisoner's *affect* is flat since his trial.

effect, *n.* the result

The new drug had no *effect* on her condition.

✳

aisle a passageway between seats

The bride is the last one down the *aisle*.

isle a small island

The *Isle* of Skye is part of Scotland.

✳

amend to correct; to improve

To *amend* the situation, you must apologize.

emend to correct a manuscript

The copy editor *emends* text.

✳

ascent the way up; incline

The *ascent* was steeper than I'd remembered.

assent agreement

Do I have your *assent* to my suggestion?

✳

assay   to appraise; to analyze
   Assaying the ore shows it is uranium.
essay, *v.*   to attempt
   I *essayed* a chat with her, with no success.
essay, *n.*   a short written piece
   The *essays* of E.B. White are concise and charming.

✳

bail   to remove water
   We *bailed* for two hours, but the boat was sinking.
bale   a bundle or tightly bound package
   Bales of hay dotted the field at harvest time.

✳

bazaar   a market or fair
   The church *bazaar* is a great place to shop.
bizarre   weird; unusual
   I had *bizarre* dreams after the accident.

✳

breach   a break or gap
   We charged through the *breach* in the wall.
breach   to make a gap; to violate
   She *breached* my trust with her lies.
breech   rear part of a gun, pants (pl.)
   His costume included Dutchman's *breeches*.

✳

canvas   heavy material, often for sails
   Canvas trousers completed his outfit.
canvass   to discuss; to solicit
   I have *canvassed* the members for support.

✳

capital, *n.*   the city or seat of government
   Richmond is the *capital* of Virginia.

capitol, *n.*   the building where a state's Congress meets
  His portrait hangs in the *capitol*.

Capitol, *n.*   the U.S. capitol building in Washington, D.C.
  The *Capitol* is a large, white, domed building.

capital, *adj.*   wonderful; great
  Putting tarragon on salmon is a *capital* idea.

capital, *n./adj.* uppercase
  Pearl had to wear a *capital* A on her dress.

capital, *n.*   relating to financial assets
  The museum's *capital* expenditures were enormous.

✳

cereal a breakfast food; grain
  I am allergic to many
  cereals.

serial   arranged in a
  continuous row
  A *serial* killer is among us.

✳

chord   harmonizing
  musical notes
  His words struck a
  familiar *chord* in my heart.

A cereal killer is among us.

cord   rope; string; membranes used in speaking
  Polyps on the vocal *cords* can inhibit speech.

✳

cite   to refer to; to use as evidence
  He *cited* an obscure law to prove his case.

sight   vision; seeing; appearance
  The *sight* of you in a sailor suit is hilarious.

site   location
  The new YMCA is on the *site* of the old CVS.

✳

coarse   rough, thick, not fine
He made a *coarse* joke about her mother.

course   route; plan of study
I am taking a *course* in programming this term.

✳

colonel   military rank above major
Colonel Jackson ordered the troops to disperse.

kernel   grain; small piece
There's a *kernel* of truth in his craziness.

✳

complement   to add to; to help compose
Her quiet charm *complements* his liveliness.

compliment   to say something nice about
I *complimented* her stunning dress.

✳

council, *n.*   a governing or advising body
Our tenants' *council* meets once a month.

counsel, *n.*   advice
She ignored his *counsel* and did her own thing.

counsel, *n.*   lawyer
I object: *Counsel* is badgering the witness.

counsel, *v.*   to advise
Penny *counseled* her son to avoid Larry's company.

✳

descent   the act of coming down
His *descent* from the horse was rather fast.

dissent   disagreement
If there's no *dissent*, let's adjourn for dinner.

✳

discreet   wise; self-restrained
He's *discreet* and will keep your secret.

discrete   separate; distinct
These *discrete* facts don't add up to a whole picture.

✳

elicit   to draw forth; to evoke
His speech *elicited* roars of approval.

illicit   illegal
Much *illicit* activity goes on in boarding schools.

✳

fair   right; just
One hundred dollars is a *fair* price for the bike.

fare   the cost of a ticket or ride
What's the *fare* to Grand Central?

✳

faze   to upset; to cause to falter
Another houseguest doesn't *faze* me.

phase   part of a cycle; aspect
What *phase* of the project are you managing?

✳

foreword   introduction to a book, etc.
The *foreword* often discusses a book's contents.

forward   ahead in time or space
He marched *forward* at the head of his troops.

✳

forth   ahead; out
The hellish legion sallied *forth*.

fourth   after third in a series
John is the *fourth* son in his family.

✳

gibe   to scoff; to joke
The other children *gibed* at his accent.

jibe   sailing term: to change course
The boom hit Sally when we *jibed*.

✳

hardy   sturdy; healthy
A *hardy* lad with an axe stood in the doorway.

hearty   cordial; friendly
She gave us a *hearty* greeting, kissing us both.

✳

hail, *v.*   to greet; to salute enthusiastically
Hail to the chief!

hail, *n.*   frozen water from the sky
Hail beat on my windshield as I drove.

hale   healthy, well
I'm happy to see you *hale* and hearty again.

✳

hall   gathering place, passageway
We met in the great *hall* to hear the speaker.

haul   to drag, to pull
I've *hauled* nearly a cord of wood this morning.

✳

hoard to save; to store away
The miser *hoarded* his money.

horde a large contingent or group
Hordes of angry shoppers
stormed the store.

✳

hole an empty space
There's a *hole* in the bucket.

whole entire
I can't believe I ate the *whole*
thing.

✳

I can't believe I ate the
hole thing.

idle   not busy, doing nothing
The devil finds work for *idle* hands.

idol   picture or sculpture of a deity
The *idol* had a threatening expression and blue eyes.

idyll   a romantic poem or experience
Tennyson's *Idylls of the King* is lovely but long.

✳

incite (in·SITE) to urge on; to encourage
The strict rules only *incited* us to rebel.

insight (IN·site) understanding
She shows great *insight* in dealing with her stepson.

✳

it's   contraction for *it is* or *it has*
It's been my pleasure to show you around.

its   possessive pronoun
The sofa was soft; I sank into *its* cushions.

✳

knew   had knowledge of
I *knew* Susan was Amy's best friend.

new   recently made or acquired
Is that a *new* cell phone?

✳

lama   a Tibetan Buddhist priest
The Dalai *Lama* is the religious leader of Tibet.

llama   an animal of the camel family
Llamas live primarily in South America.

✳

lead   a heavy metal
My heart felt like a *lead* weight.

led   was the leader; went first
He *led* his family over the mountains to safety.

✳

lightening   growing lighter
   Thank you for *lightening* my heavy load.
lightning   electrical discharge
   A bolt of *lightning* split the tree in two.

✳

mantel   shelf above a fireplace
   You'll find the matches on the *mantel*.
mantle   a cloak or covering
   The king's *mantle* was of royal purple.

✳

maze   an intricate network, puzzle
   The house is a *maze* of rooms and hallways.
maize   a type of corn
   Maize was a staple of Native American food.

✳

medal   a small object, usually metal
   He was awarded a *medal* for heroism.
meddle   to interfere
   Please don't *meddle* in my affairs.

✳

naval   pertaining to the Navy
   There's a *naval* base in Newport News.
navel   umbilicus, belly button
   The belly dancer wore a ruby in her *navel*.

✳

ordinance   a regulation, rule
   A city *ordinance* requires you to leash your dog.
ordnance   weapons of the military
   Ordnance must be safely stored on the base.

✳

palate   roof of mouth; taste or inclination
We have food to please every *palate*.

palette   painter's board; range of colors
These pants come in a *palette* of pastel colors.

pallet   crude bed; platform to hold items
Pallets loaded with canned goods filled the shelves.

✷

peak   top or summit
He's at the *peak* of his career.

peek   a brief look, glance
A *peek* at the baby assured me she was asleep.

pique   hurt vanity, resentment
His fit of *pique* at not being chosen was intense.

✷

peace   calm, the absence of war
Paying my debts gave me *peace* of mind.

piece   part; portion
I gave Gerald a *piece* of my mind for his rudeness.

✷

pedal   operate a lever to create motion
I *pedaled* 20 miles on my old bicycle.

peddle   to sell, usually traveling
He *peddled* his wares at flea markets.

✷

precede   to occur or come before
I *precedes* E except after C.

proceed   to move forward or continue
Jason *proceeded* to sell nearly all of the stock.

✷

principal, *adj.* foremost or chief
My *principal* reason for resigning is the commute.

principal, *n.*   head of school
   I was sent to the *principal's* office.
principal, *n.*   money used to generate interest
   He'd rather starve than spend the *principal*.
principle   rule; ethical consideration
   Everyone agreed this pope was a man of *principle*.

✳

raise   to lift or make higher
   If we *raise* the ceiling, the room will feel bigger.
raze   to destroy
   The Mongols *razed* the city to the ground.

✳

rain   wet weather
   Twelve days of *rain* ruined my pansies.
reign   to rule
   Queen Victoria *reigned* for more than 60 years.
rein   strap to control a horse
   Don't pull so hard on the *reins*.

✳

retch   to gag or vomit
   The terrible smell made me *retch*.
wretch   bad or miserable person
   The *wretch* had robbed his own sister's house.

✳

stationary   immobile; not moving
   The North Star appears *stationary* in the night sky.
stationery   writing paper
   His *stationery* is monogrammed with his initials.

✳

their   belonging to them
   It's *their* turn to host the Fourth of July picnic.

there   in that place
Put the mushrooms *there* on the cutting board.
they're   contraction for *they are*
I hear *they're* moving to North Carolina.

✳

troop   military unit, usually plural
Give the *troops* extra rations and a day of rest.
troupe   theatrical group
A traveling *troupe* brought *Cats* to our theatre.

✳

vain   conceited; useless
He pleaded for mercy, but his cries were *vain*.
vein   vessel through which blood flows
The nurse put the needle into a *vein* in my arm.

✳

waist, *n.*   belt area on the human body
A whalebone corset guaranteed a tiny *waist*.
waste, *n.*   trash; byproducts
Waste management is a big problem for the town.
waste, *v.*   to use carelessly; to squander
Don't *waste* time trying to get that car working.

✳

your   belonging to you
I believe this is *your* wallet I found on the counter.
you're   contraction for *you are*
You're the last person I'd suspect of treason.

7

WordSet IV: Carol Wistfully Views Modish, Self-Assured New Yorkers

Carol arrived in New York and immediately felt like a serious outsider. Could you **deracinate** a person from Pimmit Run, Nebraska, population 4,000, and reinvent her as a city person? She overtipped the taxi driver, who regarded her with **contempt**. She drew back as an **unkempt** man spoke to her **incoherently**—he seemed to want money—and lugged her suitcase up three flights to the furnished room she had sublet. It was clean and attractive, and she was grateful. After unpacking, she bought food and other **indispensable** items at the convenience store on the corner, though the loud music **emanating** from the interior was **daunting**.

WHAT A **FORTUITOUS** COINCIDENCE! SHE COULD SCARCELY **CREDIT** HER GOOD LUCK—A FRIENDLY MIDWESTERNER RIGHT DOWN THE HALL

It was the Friday before Memorial Day. Her job didn't start until Tuesday. How would she pass the time? She could **cower** in her room. She could dye her hair, take a **pseudonym**—how about Cherie?—and moonlight as an exotic dancer. She could try to **eradicate** every Nebraska part of her and become a real New Yorker. That one seemed utterly out of the question. Well, exotic dancer was a little weird, too. Could homesickness **impair** your thinking?

A walk might make her feel more at home—it was more **enterprising**, anyway, than sitting in her room. She descended the stairs again. The streets **teemed** with **impeccably dressed**, **self-assured** people in a big hurry. She thought **wistfully** of slow-paced Pimmit Run. The thought was not **conducive** to peace of mind.

Her expression was **doleful** enough to **prompt** a man passing by to say, "Cheer up, sweetheart! It can't be that bad." Wrong, Carol thought. I've made a dreadful **miscalculation**. Then she realized this was **asinine** behavior. She'd been in New York about two hours, and already she was jumping to conclusions about the place and *her* place in it. She was simply lonely. With time, the feeling would **subside**.

She returned to her room. She had to admit it had somehow **assumed** a familiar air. That was good. As she started supper on her **minuscule** two-burner stove, there came a knock at the door. Who on earth? She peered through the little eye in the door. A pleasant face gazed back. **Emboldened**, she opened the door. A young woman stood there, holding a plate.

"Hi. I'm Karen, from down the hall. I made brownies for you." She was tall and slim, with a blonde ponytail nearly to her **lithe** waist. Her clogs and jeans were **modish**, but her voice was straight out of the Midwest.

"Thank you so much! I'm Carol. Please come in."

They sat down, and Carol, unable to **restrain** her curiosity, asked, "Where are you from?"

"Galion, Ohio. Does it show? Oh, well, it'd be pretty surprising if I could **morph** into a New Yorker in a month." She gave a **nonchalant** shrug.

Carol smiled. She could scarcely **credit** her good luck—a friendly Midwesterner right down the hall, almost as much of a newcomer as she herself. What a **fortuitous** coincidence! Surely it was a **harbinger** of good things to come.

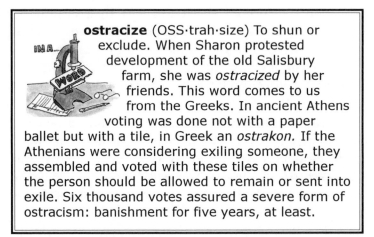

ostracize (OSS·trah·size) To shun or exclude. When Sharon protested development of the old Salisbury farm, she was *ostracized* by her friends. This word comes to us from the Greeks. In ancient Athens voting was done not with a paper ballet but with a tile, in Greek an *ostrakon.* If the Athenians were considering exiling someone, they assembled and voted with these tiles on whether the person should be allowed to remain or sent into exile. Six thousand votes assured a severe form of ostracism: banishment for five years, at least.

Carol's Words, 1st Third

deracinate (de·RASS·ih·nate´) To pull up by the roots; to uproot; to separate from a native environment or culture. A *deracinated* Parisian, he was miserable in Alaska. Carol is, understandably, experiencing culture shock in New York City after uprooting herself from her home in a tiny Nebraska town.

contempt (kun·TEMPT) Scorn; lack of respect. If you feel contempt for someone, you may believe the person is worthless; you have a low opinion of and a pronounced dislike for him or her. The word is often used with the verb hold: He was held in *contempt* by the whole town. Disregard for a judge's orders or disruptive behavior in court is a chargeable offense known as contempt of court.

unkempt (un·KEMPT) From Old English. Literally means uncombed; by extension, it means all-around messy or disheveled—shirt buttoned wrong, tie over one ear. It can also mean neglected: Your garden can be unkempt, as can your clothing. And it can mean unpolished or rough: The field workers were mostly illiterate and *unkempt*, but they worked hard.

incoherently (in·koe·HEER·unt·lee) In a rambling or disconnected manner; making little logical sense; confused or disordered. You can be incoherent with rage, grief, or excitement; if you're drunk, your speech may be incoherent. As Joshua described his fiancée, the power of his emotions rendered him *incoherent*.

indispensable (in·dih·SPEN·suh·bl) Required; essential; absolutely necessary. To lighten our load on the way up the mountain, we threw away everything that wasn't *indispensable*. Because of his strength, Sam was *indispensable* in moving all the furniture upstairs. From the same Latin root as dispenser.

emanating (EM·uh·nay´·ting) Emanate means to flow forth, to proceed, to come out: White smoke was *emanating* from the hood of the Dodge. The word works in a figurative sense also: These regulations *emanate* from a desire to protect the public. Carol is a bit put off by the store's sound system, pumping out music at some serious decibels.

daunting (DAWN·ting) Intimidating; discouraging. The verb to daunt means to discourage through fear or fatigue. I wanted to clean out the basement, but the task was *daunting*. "Nothing daunted" is an old-fashioned way of saying not frightened. Daunting's a bit shy of overwhelming, but more than a little bothersome.

cower (KOW·er) To draw back or crouch in fear; to cringe. The tiny ferret *cowered* in the corner of its cage. Thunder and lightning may cause you to cower, especially if you are out in the open. Her introduction to New York has spooked Carol so badly she feels like cowering in her room, hiding out from the fast-paced lifestyle she's glimpsed.

pseudonym (SOO·duh·nim´) From *pseudo-*, false, and *nym*, name, pseudonym means—surprise—a fictitious name. Not fictitious like Snow White: It's a name you adopt to avoid revealing your real one. Compare pseudonym with *alias*: The latter has a slightly shady feel. People tend to adopt aliases when they're stealing money or pulling scams. Pseudonyms are usually, though not always, for legitimate reasons: An author may write under a *pseudonym*; a philanthropist may do good deeds under one.

eradicate (ih·RA·dih·kate´) To destroy; to utterly ruin; to get rid of or root out. Like deracinate, eradicate comes from the Latin *radix*, meaning root, from which we also get the word radish. The Salk vaccine helped *eradicate* polio in the United States. Feeling out of place, Carol contemplates eradicating her Nebraska roots.

✸ PRACTICING CAROL'S WORDS, 1ST THIRD

The words for the first third of Carol's story are:

contempt	deracinate	indispensable
cower	emanating	pseudonym
daunting	eradicate	unkempt
	incoherently	

A. Fill in the blanks with the correct list words.

   1. The woman was dirty and _____, but she spoke like an educated person.

   2. Harriet has made herself _____; this office couldn't do without her.

   3. Cleaning up two small children's fingerpainting project is a truly _____ task.

   4. The smell_____ from the oven was delicious.

B. Which list word means disjointedly, in a rambling manner?

C. Match the list words with their correct definitions in the right-hand column.

1. cower   a. scorn

2. contempt   b. shrink or crouch in fear

3. pseudonym   c. fictitious name

D. Two list words come from the Latin word for root. The first means to pull up by the roots, the second, to root out or destroy. What are they?

E. Complete the following story with list words.

My truly (intimidating) task was to make Jane's (messy, neglected) front yard into a garden. She said I was (vitally necessary), the only one who could (uproot) the dandelions, (root out) the weeds, and plant the flowers. I wanted to (cringe) and beg off; I felt like hiding away under a (fictitious name); I even tried to refuse (in a confused, disordered way) but the (lack of respect) I felt (issuing forth) from her stopped me. I had to do it whether I liked it or not.

Answers

A. 1. unkempt; 2. indispensable; 3. daunting; 4. emanating

B. incoherently

C. 1. b; 2. a; 3. c

D. deracinate; eradicate

E. daunting; unkempt; indispensable; deracinate; eradicate; cower; pseudonym; incoherently; contempt; emanating

---

Please Don't Say That!

nuclear (NOO·klee·uhr, NYOO·klee·uhr) Pertaining to or involving atomic energy or weapons; of or relating to the nucleus, a basic part of a cell. I don't care if a sitting U.S. president said it, the word is not NOO·kyuh·lur. My *Merriam-Webster Collegiate Dictionary* tells me that this pronunciation is "disapproved of by many." That's good enough for me.

Carol's Words, 2nd Third

impair (im·PARE) To damage or weaken; to cause to become worse or less effective. Drinking *impairs* one's driving performance. Don't *impair* your health by eating trans fats. The verb may be used intransitively: She cared for her sister, *impaired* from birth. Carol is afraid she's not thinking clearly, as homesickness has impaired her mind.

enterprising (EN·ter·pry´·zing) Resourceful; venturesome; showing initiative, energy, and readiness to undertake a task or project. We are seeking *enterprising* young men and women to staff the office in Mumbai. Carol feels the need to do something more enterprising than just sitting in her room. The word *entrepreneur*, one who undertakes a venture, usually in business, is of the same derivation.

teemed (TEEMD) The verb to teem means to swarm; to abound. If a forest teems with wildlife, there are *a lot* of wild things in those woods. A marketplace that teems with pushcart vendors has an abundance of t-shirt carts. The word derives from a Middle English term for producing offspring, so it carries an undertone of fertility.

impeccably (im·PEK·uh·blee) Perfectly; flawlessly; spotlessly. If you're impeccably dressed, your outfit is perfect for the occasion and ketchup-free as well. The adjective is impeccable, which one dictionary defines it as "supremely excellent"; you may have impeccable credentials, standards, or manners. The word comes from the Latin word for sin and the prefix *in-*, meaning not, so it carries a connotation of sinlessness as well.

self-assured (self´-a·SHOORD) You can probably figure this one out with no help. It means poised, sure of oneself and—wait for it!—the way you feel when you've got a great vocabulary. Compare its synonym, *confident*. At a glance, Carol thinks the crowds on the street look very sure of themselves. Models try to project a self-assured air. Note for the record that self- words are always hyphenated.

wistfully (WIST·full·ee) Yearningly; in a manner full of longing, with some thoughtful sadness mixed in. Its 18th-century derivation blends *wishfully* with the obsolete *wistly*, meaning intently. The little boy gazed *wistfully* into the candy-store window. The word is often associated with nostalgia for what one has no longer: I thought *wistfully* of my little house on Sohier Avenue.

conducive (kun·DOO·siv, kun·DYOO·siv) Tending to help or promote. The atmosphere at the little café was *conducive* to artistic expression. The Latin root is *ducere*, to lead—hence the related word conduct: May I *conduct* (lead) you to your seat? Thinking about her hometown so far away is not going to lead to Carol's peace of mind.

doleful (DOLE·full) Sad; cheerless; full of grief. She was feeling *doleful* because of her parents' separation. Doleful can also mean causing grief: A *doleful* letter arrived, informing us of Susan's illness. And it can mean, as it does here, expressing grief: Don Quixote was sometimes called The Knight of the *Doleful* Countenance. Carol's face shows how blue she's feeling.

prompt (PROMPT) As used here, the verb means to cause someone to act. A related meaning is to assist: The man in the box onstage *prompts* actors if they forget their lines. As you probably know, the adjective prompt means punctual or on time. Diane is always *prompt*; we won't have to wait for her. It also means done without delay. The bride issued *prompt* thank-you notes for all her presents. A useful word all around.

miscalculation (mis·kal´·kyu·LAY·shun) An incorrect judgment or estimate. I fell because of a slight *miscalculation*: I thought the tree was just a foot or two from the porch. The verb is to miscalculate. The prefix *mis-* means bad or wrong, and *calculate* means to add up.

asinine (ASS·uh·nine´) Literally, like an ass or donkey; silly; foolish; unintelligent. I can't believe you'd make such an *asinine* remark. Carol's angry with herself for behaving like a simpleton. You can also use the word in its literal sense: She has an *asinine* profile. The vet treated his *asinine* patient with penicillin.

subside (sub·SIDE) To sink or fall to the bottom; in a figurative sense, to settle down; to quiet down; to lessen. The commotion *subsided* only when we played the children's favorite DVD. The flood *subsided* enough so people could safely reenter their houses. Carol hopes her feelings of loneliness will diminish in time.

✳ PRACTICING CAROL'S WORDS, 2ND THIRD

The words for the second third of Carol's story are:

asinine	impair	self-assured
conducive	impeccably	subside
doleful	miscalculation	teemed
enterprising	prompt	wistfully

A. Which sentence uses the word *conducive* correctly?

1. Mrs. Tilledge's Persian cat was conducive to a dream.

2. You were too conducive to Jason and hurt his feelings.

3. The air seems conducive this morning.

4. Frequent brushing is conducive to good dental health.

B. Popular is to friendly as successful is to _____ .

C. Fill in the blanks with the correct list words.

1. The streets _____ with sailors just off the Navy ships.

2. _____ attired, the young man set off for the interview.

3. I am delighted that his fever is beginning to _____ .

4. Through some _____, we overcharged you for the room.

5. Though she appeared _____, Belle was sensitive and vulnerable.

6. "I'd love to see Grandma again," sighed Tracy _____ .

D. Which list word is the closest synonym for the verb *damage*?

E. Match the list words with their correct definitions in the right-hand column.

1. self-assured   a. confident, poised

2. asinine   b. sad, cheerless

3. prompt   c. silly, foolish

4. doleful   d. assist, cause action

F. Complete the following story with list words.

(Longingly) I gazed at the receding car's taillights. Jonathan was gone—a (cheerless) thought not (leading) to comfort. I thought it would (worsen) my whole summer to have him gone, though it was (resourceful) of him to find work in Maine. He was so (perfectly) groomed and so (confident) he could get any job, I mused. That thought was enough to (cause) tears that wouldn't (lessen) for a while. What a childish, (foolish) (error in judgment) to think he wouldn't want to spend the summer without me!

Answers

A. 4

B. enterprising

C. 1. teemed; 2. impeccably; 3. subside; 4. miscalculation; 5. self-assured; 6. wistfully

D. impair

E. 1. a; 2. c; 3. d; 4. b

F. Wistfully; doleful; conducive; impair; enterprising; impeccably; self-assured; prompt; subside; asinine; miscalculation

Carol's Words, 3rd Third

assumed (a·SOOMD) The verb to assume has many meanings. In this case, it means to take on, put on, or be endowed with: Carol's room has taken on a familiar air. Assume can also mean take for granted without asking: I *assume* everybody wants mayonnaise. It can mean to seize or usurp without right: John *assumed* the throne while Richard was away on a crusade. And it can mean to pretend: Sally *assumed* an air of innocence.

minuscule (MIN·us·kyool´) Extremely small; tiny. The *minuscule* white dot on the horizon proved to be a sail. Carol's stove is minuscule, for a stove. Don't be fooled into thinking the word is derived from *mini*-, though that would seem to make sense. You'll spell it wrong. It actually comes from *minus*, less.

emboldened (em·BOLE·dend) Obviously derived from bold, the verb embolden means to make bold; to fill with courage. *Emboldened* by her friendly expression, I asked to look at her map. A tot of rum *emboldened* even the most faint-hearted sailors. Carol is encouraged by her view, through the peephole, of a nice-looking person.

lithe (LYTHE [*th* as in *that*]) Moving and bending with ease; flexible; graceful. Acrobats and dancers are lithe: Their limbs are supple and they move with grace. An elephant's trunk is lithe, or limber. People's limbs can also be pliant and graceful, as is Karen's waist.

modish (MOE·dish) Used of clothing, style, manners: fashionable, up-to-date, or, to put it as the French do, *au courant*, according to the current style. The French expression *à la mode* (see page 127) also means according to the latest fashion, but as you probably know, also means "served with ice cream." Don't ask.

restrain (rih·STRANE) To hold back; to suppress; or to keep in check. If you restrain yourself, you curb your impulse to do something: I *restrained* my desire to smack her for her rudeness. Before the race, the high-strung horse had to be *restrained*. It can also mean to restrict: The United States formerly *restrained* trade with China. Carol can't suppress her curiosity about her new acquaintance.

morph (MORF) To transform, or to change form. You can morph an object, as by computer: I can use the CAD CAM program to *morph* this garage into a two-story wing. The garage is being morphed. Or you can simply morph into something else: The reputable and fastidious Dr. Jekyll *morphed* into the uncouth and violent Mr. Hyde.

nonchalant (non´·sha·LAHNT) Calm; composed; apparently unconcerned. From the French words for not warm. In other words, cool. If I am nonchalant, nothing ruffles my smooth exterior. I am cool and collected. Karen's indifferent shrug conveys her lack of concern. Nonchalant means, as they say, it's all like, whatever.

credit (CREH·dit) Credit has many meanings, many to do with business and finance. You probably know a lot of them. But note that the verb to credit can mean to believe or put confidence in, to trust, to have faith in. I can't *credit* his story about surviving in Antarctica. We get the word *incredible* and its opposite, *credible*, or believable, from the same root word.

fortuitous (fore·TYEW·ih·tuss) This adjective originally meant simply by chance. Today it is most often used to mean lucky or fortunate. A few critics frown, but the rest of us are fine with it, so go ahead and use it in this positive sense. How *fortuitous* that he was going in my direction and could offer me a ride! You won't go wrong using the phrase in Carol's story—"fortuitous coincidence"—it's almost a cliché.

IN A...

fell swoop Shakespeare's phrase meaning all at once, as if by one blow. The deadly poison killed all the cattle at one *fell swoop*. Fell means cruel or deadly; as used here, it has nothing to do with falling.

---

harbinger (HAR·bin·jer) A herald; someone or something that goes before to spread news of another's approach: The robin is the *harbinger* of spring. A harbinger foreshadows a future event: Those cirrus clouds are *harbingers* of a change in the weather. Carol hopes her good luck foreshadows a happy future.

✸ PRACTICING CAROL'S WORDS, 3RD THIRD

The words for the last third of Carol's story are:

assumed	harbinger	modish
credit	lithe	morph
emboldened	minuscule	nonchalant
fortuitous		restrain

A. Fill in the blanks with the correct list words.

1. _____ by his praise for my short story, I sent the author my autobiography.

2. When they said she'd won the lottery, she could hardly _____ the good news.

3. The ballerina's _____ body is maintained by diet, exercise, and hours of practice.

4. When the song ended, we couldn't _____ our applause.

B. Which list word is the closest antonym for *enormous*?

C. Match the list words with their correct definitions in the right-hand column.

1. fortuitous   a. taken on

2. modish   b. stylish

3. assumed   c. calm, indifferent

4. nonchalant   d. fortunate

D. 1. Which list word might be used in describing a caterpillar's life cycle?

2. Which list word might describe a "herald angel"?

E. Complete the following story with list words.

The girls, (filled with courage), couldn't (hold back) their excitement when they saw the (fashionable) collection of hats. They modeled each and (put on) the (cool and collected) airs of sophisticated ladies. One (very small), (graceful) girl seemed to (change) into a grande dame. I could hardly (believe) her performance. It was (fortunate) that I had my camera.

Answers

A. 1. emboldened; 2. credit; 3. lithe; 4. restrain

B. minuscule

C. 1. d; 2. b; 3. a; 4. c

D. 1. morph; 2. harbinger

E. emboldened; restrain; modish; assumed; nonchalant; minuscule; lithe; morph; credit; fortuitous

A Strategem for Learning the Meanings of New Words: Prefixes, Roots, and Suffixes

Here's an easy way to make an educated guess at the meaning of an unfamiliar word. It's estimated that more than half our English words are derived in part or in full from Greek and Latin. So it makes sense to gain some familiarity with the Greek and Latin word parts that make up this large number. If you know what a root (main body of a word), a prefix (at the beginning of a word), or a suffix (at the end), or all three mean, it's often easy to figure out the meaning of a word without googling Merriam-Webster online.

For example, take the word *bicyclist* and pretend for a moment you don't know what it means. If you know the prefix *bi-* means two, the root *cyclo-* means circular, and the suffix *-ist* means one who does, you can take a guess that a bicyclist is someone who does something on two circles, or wheels—that is, a bike. Hm. Maybe you have to have some intuition, or inspiration, too. Here's an easier one: *rhinitis*. If you know that *rhino-* is the prefix for nose, and *-itis* is a suffix meaning inflammation, you can dope out that rhinitis is a nose inflammation, or a cold. How cool is that?

Here are some prefixes frequently used in English, with meanings and examples. Become familiar with them and you'll have a significant tool to use in building your vocabulary.

Common Prefixes

Prefix	Meaning	Examples
a-, an-	without, not	apolitical, arrhythmia, anarchy
ab-	away from	abnormal, absent
acro-	high, height	acrobat, acrophobia
ad-	both	adhere, adjust, adjoin
ambi-	to, toward	ambidextrous, ambiguous
ante-	before	antebellum, antecedent
anti-	against	antidote, antiseptic
astro-	star	astronomy, astrology
audio-	listening	audiotape, audiovisual
auto-	self	autopilot, automatic
bene-	good	benefit, benevolent
bi-	two	bicycle, bilingual
bio-	life, living thing	biology, biography
cardio-	heart	cardiovascular, cardiogram
centi-	hundred	centennial, cent
circum-	around	circumnavigate, circumference
co-	together, with	cooperate, co-host
com-, con-	together, with	compile, contact
contra-	against	contradict, contrary
counter-	against, opposite	counteract, counterfeit
de-	down, away, out of	descend, deflate, defrost
dec-	ten	decade, decimal
dis-	not, not any, absence	discomfort, disease
dys-	sick, difficult, bad	dysfunction, dyslexia, dystrophy

Prefix	Meaning	Examples
e-	from, out of	eject, edit, elect
em-, en-	cover, cause, into	emphasize, empower, ennoble
epi-	upon	epidermis, epitome
equi-	equal	equidistant, equivalent
eu-	well, good	eulogy, euthanasia
ex-	without, outside	excavate, exhale, exit
extra-	beyond, out of	extraordinary, extravagant
fore-	before	foregoing, foremost, foreword
geo-	earth, geography	geology, geophysics, geopolitics
hemi-	half	hemiplegia, hemisphere
hetero-	different	heterodox, heterosexual
homo-	same	homonym, homosexual
hydro-	water	hydrate, hydraulic, hydropower
hyper-	over, overly	hyperactive, hypersensitive
hypno-	sleep	hypnotherapy, hypnotize
hypo-	under	hypothermia, hypoacidity
il-	not	illegal, illiberal, illicit
im-, in-	not	imperfect, improbable, incredible, infirm
im-, in-	into	imbibe, immigrate, inroads, inter
inter-	between	intercept, international, intertwine
intra-	within	intrastate, intravenous
intro-	in, inward	introduce, introspective

Prefix	Meaning	Examples
ir-	not	irrational, irreverent
kilo-	thousand	kilogram, kilometer
macro-	great, large	macrobiotic, macrocosm
mal-, male-	bad, evil	malefactor, malignant
mega-	million	megabucks, megahertz, megavitamin
meta-	beyond	metaphor, metaphysical
micro-	small	microorganism, microprocessor
milli-	thousandth	millennium, millimeter
mini-	small	miniature, miniskirt
mis-	bad, wrong	misdemeanor, misprint
mono-	one, single	monorail, monotonous
neo-	new	neoconservative, neonate, neophyte
neuro-	nerve	neuropathy, neurotic
non-	not	nonsense, nonviolent
ob-	against, to	obstacle, obstruct
pan-	every, all	panorama, Pan-American
para-	beside, abnormal, resembling	paraphernalia, paraphrase, paraplegic
patri-	father	paternity, patriot
per-	through	permeate, perennial, peruse
peri-	around	perimeter, peripheral
phil-, philo-	like, love	philanthropy, philosopher
phon-, phono-	sound	phonics, phonograph
photo-	light	photoactive, photograph

Prefix	Meaning	Examples
phys-	body, nature	physical, physics
poly-	numerous	polygamous, polygon
post-	after	postscript, postwar
pre-	before	pre-approve, prelude
pro-	forward, in favor of	progress, produce, promote
proto-	first, earliest	protoplasm, prototype
pseudo-	false	pseudonym, pseudopregnancy
psycho-	mind	psychology, psychotic
radio-	radiation	radiography, radiology
re-	again, back	repeat, rerun, return
retro-	backward	retroactive, retrofit
rhino-	nose	rhinoceros, rhinitis
se-	apart, away	secede, secluded
semi-	half	semiannual, semicircle
sex-	six	sextet, sextuplets
sub-	under	submarine, subordinate, subway
super-	upon, above	superintendent, supernova
sym-, syn-	with, together	symphony, synonym, synthesis
tele-	distant	telephone, telescope
tetra-	four	tetrapod, tetrarch
therm-, thermo-	heat	thermodynamics, thermometer
trans-	across	transatlantic, transportation
tri-	three	triangle, tricycle
ultra-	beyond, very	ultraviolet, ultrasensitive
un-	not	unknown, unusual
uni-	one	unicorn, unilateral

Some Familiar Roots

A Latin or Greek root may be joined by a prefix, a suffix, and/or another root. There are hundreds of roots: The ones listed here are just a very few common ones. A good dictionary (not just a pocket version) will give you the root of a word, along with the prefixes and suffixes involved, if any. It's fun to see where our words came from. For example, I bet you didn't know that fierce and treacle (a sickeningly sweet syrup used in England) come to us from the root *-ghwer-*. Amazing.

Root	Meaning	Examples
-anthrop-	human	anthropology, philanthropy
-chron-	time	anachronism, chronicle, synchronize
-dem-	people	democracy, demographics, pandemic
-dict-	to say	contradiction, dictator
-duc-	to lead, to bring	deduction, produce
-fer-	to carry	confer, transference
-fix-	to fasten	prefix, suffix
-graph-	to write	photograph, polygraph
-gress-	to walk	egress, progress
-ject-	to throw	eject, reject
-jur-, -just-	law	jurisprudence, justice
-log-, -logue-	word, speech	biology, monologue, prologue
-luc-	light	elucidate, translucent
-manu-	hand	manual, manufacture
-meter-	measure	kilometer, thermometer

Root	Meaning	Examples
-op-, -oper-	work	cooperate, opera
-path-	feeling, suffering	empathy, sympathy
-ped-	foot	centipede, pedestrian
-pel-	to drive	compel, repel
-pend-	to hang	depend, suspend
-port-	to carry	import, support
-scrib-	to write	describe, manuscript, subscribe
-tract-	to pull, to drag	attract, tractor
-vac-	empty	vacation, vacuum
-vert-	to turn	convert, divert
-vid-, -vis-	to see	revise, television, video

In 3 Words: The Rule of 3

While we're on the subject of using words well, here's something you should know. People like to read about groups of three: the butcher, the baker, and the candlestick maker; gold, frankincense, and myrrh; the Three Bears, the Three Little Pigs, the Three Musketeers. Trilogies. Three seems to satisfy some kind of inner geometry.

This principle carries over into writing. When we organize, we do it in threes: We write about the beginning, the middle, and the end; the past, present, and future; we tell them what we're going to tell them, we tell them, then we tell them what we told them.

You could do a lot worse than remember this rule when you organize a proposal, an article, or any piece of writing. (Look at that: Three types of written work, and I wasn't even thinking about it. It's probably automatic with you as well.)

Common Suffixes

Suffixes come at the right-hand end of a word. They determine the role of a word; that is, they determine the function of a word in a sentence. The root word *art*, for example, becomes *artist* with the addition of the suffix *-ist*, which means one who. And you can make adverbs by adding *-ly* to almost any adjective: mad, madly; verbal, verbally. Some familiar suffixes follow. There are many, many more.

Suffix	Meaning or Function	Examples
-able, -ible	forms adjectives; able to or worthy of	allowable, reachable, lovable
-al	forms adjectives	mental, trivial
-ance, -ence	forms nouns	performance, audience
-ant	one who causes	claimant, informant
-ate	forms verbs	celebrate, operate
-ation	forms nouns; condition or state	fixation, realization
-cide	forms nouns; killer	insecticide, suicide
-dom	forms nouns; condition or state	freedom, wisdom
-ectomy	surgical removal of	appendectomy, tonsillectomy
-en	forms verbs; to make	happen, quicken
-er	forms nouns	driver, viewer
-fy, -ify	forms nouns; act or state	purify, specify
-hood	forms adjective; dealing with	neighborhood, statehood
-ia, -y	forms verbs	dyslexia, aristocracy
-ic, -ical	forms nouns, adjectives	comic, logical, tonic

Suffix	Meaning or Function	Examples
-ics	having to do with	economics, politics
-ism	state of, theory of	Judaism, pessimism
-ist	one who	activist, Communist
-ite	forms nouns; one connected with	meteorite, socialite
-ity, -ty	forms nouns	ability, versatility
-ize	forms verbs	capitalize, modernize
-gram	an image or record	electrocardiogram, sonogram
-logy	field, study	geology, sociology
-ment	forms nouns	arrangement, management
-ness	forms nouns	carelessness, fitness
-oid	like, shape	android, spheroid
-or	forms nouns; one who	actor, spectator
-phobia	fear	claustrophobia, agoraphobia
-tic	forms adjectives	elastic, fantastic
-sis	state of, condition of	analysis, basis

Please Don't Say That!

mischievous (MIS·chih·vuss) The word means playfully naughty. It is *not* pronounced mis·CHEE·vee·uss. Why on earth would it be? Just look: There's no *I* after the *v*. Remember that *mispronouncing* a word can make you look just as bad as using the wrong one. Always check your dictionary if you're not sure how to pronounce a word.

By the way, don't feel bad if you don't recognize the example words: A lot of them are specialized and difficult. If you look at the root words along with their prefixes and suffixes, however, you'll have a good shot at figuring out the meanings. *Techno*- plus *phobia*, for instance—you'd have no problem guessing correctly that it's fear of technology.

WordSet V: Tumultuous Rapture: Lawrence Is Infatuated With a Beguiling Bride

Lawrence was **anticipating** the wedding with pleasure even though he knew few people besides the groom. He'd broken off a long-term relationship 11 months ago. The pain had begun to **recede** after a few months as he realized he'd been more **infatuated** than in love with Faye. In recent weeks he'd been wishing someone special would enter his life. He recalled the old Irish superstition that going to a wedding would bring on another. Maybe he'd meet her at this one. In the **interim**, his life was going well, and he was happy that Jonathan, at least, had found his life's companion.

The plane landed in Santa Fe with a hearty thump, and the passengers cheered. Lawrence **hailed** a cab and within half an hour was **ensconced** in his hotel room. He watched the news, then changed clothes and, no longer **encumbered** with luggage, took a cab to the church. He hadn't **reckoned** on its nearness to the hotel and arrived quite early. **Ambling** around in search of a water fountain, he descended a flight of stairs and found himself in a **labyrinth** of small rooms. As he passed an open doorway, he suddenly locked eyes with a beautiful girl sitting on a sofa, dressed in yards of white lace. The bride! He couldn't remember her name, which was **mortifying**. But they somehow began to **converse** without introductions and without **constraint**. In addition to being witty and **erudite**, she **exuded** a **beguiling serenity**, while her eyes hinted at a **latent frivolity**. Lucky Jonathan, he thought with a **scintilla** of pure envy. It was **appalling**: He'd fallen in love at first sight, and with his best friend's bride.

But he was **mystified**. "Why are you sitting here alone?" he couldn't **refrain** from asking. It was, after all, probably the most **momentous** day

THEY BEGAN TO **CONVERSE** WITHOUT INTRODUCTIONS AND WITHOUT **RESTRAINT**

of her life so far. And weren't there things brides needed to do before the ceremony? Wasn't she being missed?

She gestured with a ringless left hand. "Actually, the whole wedding thing was starting to be too much. I just needed to get away for a bit."

Wanting to give her space, he tried to **quell** his new feelings and reluctantly excused himself. He took a seat as the church began to fill with guests. He told himself it was **arrant** nonsense to fall in love with a bride on her wedding day, but his emotions were so **tumultuous** as to be nearly **intolerable**.

The **soporific** organ prelude gave way to a joyous march. A small girl came down the aisle scattering red rose petals, her white lace dress a tiny **replica** of the one he'd just seen. Then, the bride herself—but what was going on? There were four women, all dressed in identical white lace gowns! And last, a woman on her father's arm, **arrayed** in **tier** upon tier of dazzling *red* lace—the bride. The effect was stunning. Suddenly he understood: The four girls in white were bridesmaids, his angel among them. He experienced a moment of pure **rapture**. Only a bridesmaid, and not even an engagement ring on her finger! From the **chancel**, she flashed him a quick smile. Things were definitely looking up.

Lawrence's Words, 1st Third

anticipating (an·TIH·sih·pate´·ing) The verb anticipate means to expect, to await, or to foresee: I don't *anticipate* any problems with the sale. It can also mean to look forward to with pleasure: He *anticipated* a lovely afternoon of hiking and swimming. Among quite a few other possible meanings, it can have the sense of preventing by acting beforehand: He *anticipated* my objection by explaining that the meeting was just a formality.

recede (rih·SEED) To retreat; to draw back; to move away: The flood waters *receded*, and we were able to return to our homes. The word can be used literally or figuratively to mean become faint or distant: My memories of the fire gradually *receded* as I grew older. Lawrence's anguish over his lost love has diminished.

infatuated (in·FA·choo·ate´·ed) Filled with an irrational, quite possibly temporary, passion. She's so *infatuated* with her new friend that she has no time for us. He's *infatuated* with snowboarding. There's an element of foolishness involved in infatuation; in fact, the word comes from the Latin *fatuus*, which means foolish. Lawrence contrasts being infatuated with being truly in love.

interim (IN·tuh·ruhm) A period of time between one event, period, or process and another: the interim between the two world wars, for example, or the interim between a divorce and remarriage. As an adjective, interim means temporary: The Socialists formed an *interim* government.

hailed (HAYLD) The verb to hail primarily means to cheer, to salute, or to greet: We *hailed* the winner of the gymnastics competition. *Hail* to the chief. It can also mean, as it does here, to call or call for, to attract attention by calling out: You can hail a waiter or a friend as well as a cab.

ensconced (en·SKONSD) Securely or snugly settled. People in books seem always to be ensconced in cozy armchairs. Lawrence is safely tucked into his hotel room. The verb to ensconce may also mean to conceal or hide: We found the candlesticks *ensconced* in a small space beneath the floorboards.

encumbered (en·KUM·burd) To encumber is to burden; encumbered accordingly means burdened, or carrying a heavy load. Lawrence has left his suitcase and carry-on bag at the hotel and is now *un*encumbered. Encumbered can also mean restricted or hindered: I was so *encumbered* by the red tape my job involved that I could get nothing done. And you can be encumbered with debt or family obligations.

reckoned (REH·kund) To reckon means to calculate or compute; to count on: I hadn't *reckoned* the cost of an evening in Paris. Lawrence hasn't included in his calculation how close the church is to the hotel. To reckon with is to deal with: His mother-in-law is a force to be *reckoned* with. Except with close friends and family, don't use reckon as a synonym for think: I *reckon* Betsy's gone to Boston. It's a little too informal.

ambling (AM·bling) The verb to amble means to walk in a leisurely fashion, to stroll. When you amble, you aren't particularly full of purpose; you may be taking a walk without a destination, or you may just be taking your time: *Ambling* around the park, I noticed a lot of litter. Lawrence is strolling around, hoping to find a water fountain, but also just killing time.

labyrinth (LAB·ih·rinth) An intricate set of paths and passages; a maze: The hacienda was a *labyrinth* of rooms opening off other rooms. Any intricate puzzle or complicated, bewildering state of things or events: Charlene's weekend plans were a *labyrinth* of contradictory happenings. Lawrence has probably found his way into the parish hall basement and an assortment of Sunday School classrooms.

mortifying (MORE·tih·fye´·ing) To mortify is to cause (someone) to feel shame or humiliation. It's a strong word, coming as it does from the Latin *mortificare*, to put to death. Doesn't get much stronger than that, so you'd think it would only apply in extreme situations. We tend, however, to use it rather casually—for embarrassing moments, for example: I was *mortified* that she caught me in my little white lie about the dinner party.

✹ PRACTICING LAWRENCE'S WORDS, 1ST THIRD

The words for the first third of Lawrence's story are:

ambling	hailed	labyrinth
anticipating	infatuated	mortifying
ensconced	interim	recede
encumbered	reckoned	

A. Fill in the blanks with the correct list words.

1. John tried to help Sarah up the hill, but, _____ with his camping gear, he wasn't much use.

2. Under the town was an intricate_____ of tunnels for servicing water and sewer pipes.

3. When I finally saw Althea coming up the hill, I _____ her with joy and relief.

4. When we got to the club, we found Nicky _____ in an armchair, eating pretzels.

B. Galloping is to trotting as striding is to _____.

C. Which sentence uses the word *recede* correctly?

1. The electricity is turned off; you may recede with the repair of the refrigerator.

2. The rain ruined the garden, and I had to recede the whole thing.

3. Sheryl wasn't sure of the answer and was forced to recede the meaning.

4. The farther Anna walked, the more the mountains seemed to recede into the distance.

D. Match the list words with their correct definitions in the right-hand column.

1. anticipating   a. madly in love

2. infatuated   b. figured, calculated

3. mortifying   c. humiliating

4. reckoned   d. awaiting

E. Which list word is the closest synonym for *meantime*?

F. Complete the following story with list words.

As I was (sauntering) down Fifth Avenue, (looking forward to) a good lunch at Marie's, a voice (called out to) me. It was a boy I'd once been (in love) with. I hadn't (figured) on his powerful effect on me. In the (time interval) since I'd seen him, I'd been very little (burdened) with thoughts of him. It was (embarrassing) to discover how quickly he caused thoughts of my new love to (retreat). If only I'd been safely (tucked) in a booth at Marie's before I saw him!

Answers

A. 1. encumbered; 2. labyrinth; 3. hailed; 4. ensconced

B. ambling

C. 4

D. 1. d; 2. a; 3. c; 4. b

E. interim

F. sauntering; anticipating; hailed; infatuated; reckoned; interim; encumbered; mortifying; recede; ensconced

Lawrence's Words, 2nd Third

converse (kun·VURSS) To talk; to chat; to speak informally with one or more other persons. The noun, as you know, is conversation. Lawrence and the attractive stranger converse easily while awaiting the wedding. This is a word to use freely in any spoken or written matter, whereas a near-synonym such as *verbalize* (to put into words) is less flexible.

constraint (kun·STRAYNT) A limit or restriction; awkwardness. Lawrence is able to say just what he wants to with this young woman; he's not constrained to be super-clever, use long words, avoid certain subjects, and so forth, and he feels no awkwardness in her presence. Constraint can be used also to mean repression of natural feelings: I wanted to burst into tears, but I felt a certain *constraint* with my uncle in the room.

erudite (EHR·yew·dite´, EHR·uh·dite´) Having or displaying profound knowledge; learned; scholarly. The woman is not only gorgeous, she's knowledgeable, too—a combination irresistible to Lawrence. Coming as it does from the same root as the word *rude*, and meaning literally not rude, the word carries a connotation of polish or refinement. George W. Bush knows a lot about a lot of things, but nobody who says Artic and nucular is *erudite*.

exuded (ek·ZOOD·ed, ek·SOOD·ed) The verb is to exude, meaning to discharge; to emit; to come out gradually in small drops or bits, like toothpaste. The Latin root is *exudare*, meaning "to ooze out like sweat." Dear me—graphic, but illustrative: If you exude something, it's as if it's coming out your pores. By extension, the word means to give off, project, or display, as a quality: He absolutely *exudes* self-satisfaction. The lady in white *exudes*, or projects, serenity.

beguiling (bee·GYLE·ing) Very attractive; charming; amusing. Everyone believes their grandchildren are the most *beguiling* creatures on the planet. The word can also mean charming but in a deceitful way, influencing by trickery: Helen is *beguiling* James into spending his fortune on her. The verb is to beguile, and there's an adverb, beguilingly.

serenity (suh·REN·ih·tee) The quality of being calm or tranquil. The adjective is serene. Gee, this girl's got a lot going for her. Serenity can apply to a place as well as a person: I love the *serenity* of a mountain lake. In our busy lives, we sometimes long for serenity. The word comes from the Latin for sky or weather and originally meant clear or unclouded.

latent (LAYT·nt) Present but not visible or apparent: Suzanne had a *latent* desire to dance professionally. Fingerprints may be latent, visible after dusting. The word can refer to an ability that could be developed: Daniel has a *latent* ability to sing countertenor. Lawrence's new acquaintance seems like someone who could harbor some fun and silliness, though she's not expressing it.

frivolity (frih·VOLL·ih·tee) She's getting better by the minute. Frivolity can mean the quality of being trivial, foolish, and/ or self-indulgent, sort of like Marie Antoinette playing shepherdess while the French people were starving. But it's used here in its meaning of frolicsome, lighthearted, maybe even absurd behavior.

scintilla (sin·TILL·ah) A trace; a particle; a smidgen. A tiny flash or spark. There's not a *scintilla* of evidence to prove Edwin was ever present at the campsite. Lawrence can't repress a tiny flash of jealousy when he imagines his friend marrying this wonderful woman.

appalling (ah·PAWL·ing) The verb is to appall. From Old French *appalir*, to grow pale: horrifying; dismaying; dreadful; causing consternation—so upsetting it makes you pale. It's often applied to a person's appearance or behavior: His antics at Maeve's retirement party were *appalling*. To Lawrence, having fallen for his friend's bride is appalling, which makes sense.

mystified (MISS·tuh·fyde) To mystify means to bewilder, confuse, or puzzle, to throw into utter perplexity. Lawrence is mystified by the presence of the person he takes to be the bride, sitting alone in the parish hall just before her wedding. It makes no sense. I may be mystified as to why my coworker, who has a record of absenteeism, was promoted over me. You might be mystified if you received an anonymous note inviting you to a meeting in the moonlight.

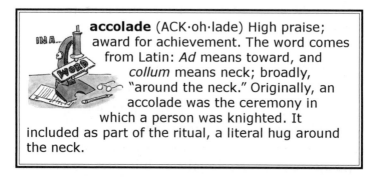

accolade (ACK·oh·lade) High praise; award for achievement. The word comes from Latin: *Ad* means toward, and *collum* means neck; broadly, "around the neck." Originally, an accolade was the ceremony in which a person was knighted. It included as part of the ritual, a literal hug around the neck.

✳ PRACTICING LAWRENCE'S WORDS, 2ND THIRD

The words for the second third of Lawrence's story are:

appalling	erudite	latent
beguiling	exuded	mystified
constraint	frivolity	scintilla
converse		serenity

A. If my spouse has lost all our money in the stock market, and I am considering a cruise and also taking flying lessons, said spouse might accuse me of _____.

B. Fill in the blanks with the correct list words.

　1. Chuck threw spitballs, refused to dance with Janet, and generally behaved in a truly _____ manner.

　2. The tree _____ a sticky sap that smelled strongly of pine.

　3. Samantha was at her most _____, flirting with the men and charming the women.

4. My nephew does poorly in school, but I believe he has _____ abilities yet to be developed.

C. Which list word is the closest antonym for *an enormous quantity*?

D. Which list word might you prefer not to do when in the dentist's chair?

E. Match the list words with their correct definitions in the right-hand column.

1. constraint	a. calm
2. erudite	b. puzzled
3. mystified	c. awkwardness
4. serenity	d. knowledgeable

F. Complete the following story with list words.

The detectives called to the case were (learned) and (projected) professionalism, but they were at first (perplexed) over Howard's murder. He was dead, but not a (tiny piece) of evidence showed how or why. They dusted for (invisible) fingerprints and tried to (talk) with all the houseguests. Belinda showed (horrible) manners, Cassandra was her usual (charming) self, full of (lighthearted behavior), Dexter displayed a certain (repression of feeling), and Max showed a surprising (calmness)—which was all the more surprising when they arrested him.

Answers

A. frivolity

B. 1. appalling; 2. exuded; 3. beguiling; 4. latent

C. scintilla

D. converse

E. 1. c; 2. d; 3. b; 4. a

F. erudite; exuded; mystified; scintilla; latent; converse; appalling; beguiling; frivolity; constraint; serenity

Lawrence's Words, 3rd Third

refrain (rih·FRANE) To resist an impulse; to hold oneself back from doing something: I will *refrain* from telling Marissa what I think of her behavior. Please don't *refrain* from giving me your honest opinion. Helena *refrained* with difficulty from hugging her 12-year-old nephew in front of his classmates. Lawrence can't resist asking the girl why she's in the church basement alone.

momentous (moe·MEN·tuss) Of huge importance or significance. Peter was about to make the most *momentous* decision of his life. Occasions are often described as momentous: a groundbreaking ceremony, the public offering of stock in a company, a bride's wedding day—all can be considered momentous. The word refers to abstractions—discoveries, periods of time, experiences—rather than items or people: Although either may be important to you, you wouldn't call a computer or a boss momentous.

quell (KWELL) To suppress or put an end to. The secret police quickly *quelled* the resistance movement. To pacify or calm: My friends tried to *quell* my fears about my upcoming audition at the music conservatory. From an Old English word meaning kill. Because he believes they're unsuitable, Lawrence is trying to kill his feelings for the unknown woman.

arrant (A·ruhnt) Utter; complete; thoroughgoing; downright. Usually used in an uncomplimentary sense: an *arrant* fool, *arrant* trickery, an *arrant* lie. Lawrence criticizes his feelings as arrant nonsense, meaning total foolishness.

tumultuous (too·MUL·choo·uhs, tyoo·MUL·choo·uhs) Filled with disturbance and uproar, even violent: the *tumultuous* events of April 1985, when revolutionists took over the capital city. Noisy or disorderly: a *tumultuous* crowd of teenagers on vacation. Troubled, agitated: Lawrence's feelings are in an uproar.

✳ 123

intolerable (in·TAHL·uh·ruh·bl) Not bearable; impossible to put up with. My ears were ringing from the *intolerable* noise of the jackhammer. You may find some modern music intolerable. Her snobbish behavior is *intolerable*: I don't want her around. Lawrence's emotions are so strong as to be almost unbearable.

soporific (sopp·uh·RIFF·ik) Tending to cause sleep, as a drug. Anything that puts you to sleep may be called soporific: I found the lecture on bromeliads *soporific*. It means sleepy or drowsy as well: my *soporific* dinner companion. The noun is soporific also: A soporific is something that causes or induces sleep, such as a sleeping pill. The organist has been playing dreamy, sleep-inducing music, as compared with the wedding marches that follow.

replica (REP·lih·kuh) A copy or reproduction; a duplicate. The copy of the *Mona Lisa* in the gallery is a *replica*. For the anniversary party, the pastry chef made a cake that was an exact *replica* of our house in meringue and marzipan. A replica is often smaller than the original. Unlike a forgery, a replica isn't intended to deceive.

arrayed (uh·RAYD) To array means to dress in fine clothes. The bride is turned out in spectacular finery. If you're arrayed, you're probably more gorgeous than if you're just attired (page 70). Zeke, cleaned up and *arrayed* in a three-piece suit, was scarcely recognizable. You met the noun *array* in Charlie's story (Chapter 1, page 11), meaning an arrangement or display, often an impressive one: An *array* of topaz necklaces and earrings in the store window caught my eye.

tier (TEER) A layer or row rising above or behind another. The rows of seats in a theater balcony can be called tiers; the layers of a cake are tiers. The bride's gown evidently features rows and rows of red lace. Let's hope she's thin; that kind of stuff is hard to wear.

rapture (RAP·cher) A state in which one is carried away by great happiness; ecstasy; joy. Lawrence experiences a moment of rapture when he realizes his newfound love is not, after all, his friend's bride. Rapture is passionate delight that overwhelms a person; it's not a calm emotion such as contentment, for example. I may be filled with rapture upon learning that a distant relative has died and left me a million dollars, or that my son has been accepted at Harvard.

chancel (CHAN·sell) The space around the altar of a church, usually in front and sometimes enclosed by a railing. This is the area in which the minister or priest conducts the church service. Sometimes the choir sits in the chancel as well. A chancel drama is a play that takes place in this area.

✺ PRACTICING LAWRENCE'S WORDS, 3RD THIRD

The words for the last third of Lawrence's story are:

arrant	momentous	replica
arrayed	quell	soporific
chancel	rapture	tier
intolerable	refrain	tumultuous

A. Match the following list words with their correct definitions in the right-hand column.

1. chancel   a. the area near a church altar

2. replica   b. row, as of seating

3. rapture   c. duplicate

4. tier   d. ecstasy

B. Which two list words, nearly antonyms, best fit the blanks? At night, one of our twins is a _____ little angel, the other makes a _____ commotion.

C. Fill in the blanks with the correct list words.

1. I tried all kinds of drugs to try to _____ the pain of my headaches.

2. On that _____ Friday, we learned the sale had finally gone through.

3. We ask that you _____ from clapping until all have received their diplomas.

4. Justine's had enough of Marcus; his cruel behavior has become _____ to her.

5. I wore a sundress; everyone else was _____ in evening gowns.

D. If someone is described as an arrant joker, he or she probably _____.

1. likes to joke a little   3. loves to joke
2. hates to joke   4. none of these

E. Fill in the blanks with the correct list words.

Brendan was hired to carve a (smaller copy) of a ship with (rows) of squaresails to hang above the (area around a church altar) at Our Lady, Star of the Sea. The congregation of fishermen broke into (noisy, unruly) applause the (very significant) Sunday when it was unveiled. The priest could not (hold back) from voicing (delight, joy). But Brendan turned out to be an (utter, complete) bad hat: he committed the (unbearable) sin of tripling his estimate for the job. No one could (suppress) the angry mob, who ran him out of town for his lack of religious feeling.

Answers

A. 1. a; 2. c; 3. d; 4. b

B. soporific, tumultuous

C. 1. quell; 2. momentous; 3. refrain; 4. intolerable;
5. arrayed

D. 3

E. replica; tiers; chancel; tumultuous; momentous; refrain; rapture; arrant; intolerable; quell

10

Foreign Words and Phrases: Understand Them! Use Them!

It can be kind of spooky when someone you're conversing with suddenly begins speaking in tongues. If you're familiar with the following foreign terms, it won't bother you a bit. In fact, they can add zip to your own conversation and writing—a certain *je ne sais quoi*, as it were.

It's interesting to see how many of these adopted words and phrases are French. Maybe it's because the French always have a word for it. They are, in fact, so good at *le mot juste* that French has only a fifth of the number of words we have in English. Cross my heart.

a capella (ah kuh·PELL·ah)
In the manner of the chapel, referring to medieval music sung in church by unaccompanied voices. An *a capella* singing group performs without instrumental accompaniment. *A capella* groups abound on college campuses, singing everything from pop music to madrigals. (Italian)

à la mode (ah lah MODE)
In the latest fashion; with ice cream. Your new hairstyle is very *à la mode*. Would you like your apple pie *à la mode*? Usually you can tell from the context which meaning is intended. It's not stylish to put ice cream in your hair, at least not yet. (French)

ad infinitum (add in´·fih·NYE·tum)
To infinity; endlessly; on and on. I thought he was going to talk about his new beach house *ad infinitum*. (Latin)

arrivederci (ah·ree·vuh·DARE·chee)
Until we meet again. (Italian)

au contraire (owe kon·TRAYRE)
On the contrary. Dislike him? *Au contraire*: I am wild about him. (French)

au courant (owe koo·RANH)
Knowledgeable; up-to-date; informed on current events. The prime minister has some background knowledge of the Tanzania situation, and constant briefings keep him *au courant*. (French)

au fait (owe FAY)
Socially correct or just right. (French)

autres temps, autres moeurs (owe·truh TAHN, owe·truh MURSS)
Other times; other customs. In other words, they used to do it this way, but nowadays it's a different story. (French)

Please Don't Say That!
vichyssoise
(vee´·shee·SWAHZ, vih´·shee·SWAHZ) Hailing from Vichy, France, this is a delicious soup, often served cold, made with potatoes, onions or leeks, and cream. People often make the mistake of not sounding the last *s*— and it *is* a mistake. You'll sound knowledgeable, if not utterly cosmopolitan, if you pronounce it as it's given here.

---

bon appétit (banh a·pay·TEE)
Enjoy! Literally, "good appetite." This is what the waiter has been saying when he sets your plate in front of you. (French)

bona fide (BAH·nah FYDE, BOE·nah FYDE, BAH·nah FYE·dee)
Made or done in good faith; genuine. This is a *bona fide* letter written by George Washington. The noun *bona fides* means sincerity or good faith. (Latin)

c'est la vie (say lah VEE)
That's life; that's the way it goes. (French)

carte blanche (kart BLANHSH)
Full power and authority to act as one sees fit; freedom to do whatever one wishes. My boss gave me *carte blanche* to deal with the McIntosh project. (French)

cherchez la femme (share·shay lah FAMM)
Look for the woman—meaning there's always a woman involved. (French)

ciao (CHOW)
An informal greeting; hi or goodbye. Interestingly, it comes from the Italian dialect word for slave—the meaning being "I am your servant." (Italian)

comme il faut (kumm eel FOE)
Proper, up to standard, just as it should be. Juliet's wedding was exactly *comme il faut*, thanks to her mother's endless hours of effort. (French)

cordon bleu (kor´·dohn BLEUH [That French *-eu* is somewhere between uh and eh. Just don't pronounce it blue.])
Of a dish made of chicken or veal, usually stuffed with ham and cheese. The words literally mean blue ribbon and may also be used to refer to a person distinguished in his or her field, especially a master chef. (French)

cul-de-sac (KULL·duh·sack)
A blind alley or dead end. It's literally a rude way of saying "bottom of the bag." I told you the French always have a word for it. (French)

de rigueur (duh ree·GURR)
Required by fashion or etiquette. In other words, don't show up without it. A gorgeous big hat is *de rigueur* at Ascot. (French)

déjà vu (day·zhah VOO)
Literally, already seen. You can apply this to something that is passé or has lost its freshness. It also applies to the eerie phenomenon most of us experience occasionally, in which you are utterly convinced you have been in the same exact conversation or situation before. (French)

Deo gratias (day´·owe GRAH·tee·ahss)
God willing. (Latin)

doppelganger (DOPP·uhl·gang´·er)
A spiritual or ghostly double or twin, often haunting its living counterpart. My long-lost brother so resembled me that I felt as if I were seeing my *doppelganger*. (German)

double entendre (DUB·uhl ahn·TAHN·druh, DOOBL ahn·TANH·druh)
Double meaning. A phrase that may be taken two ways, usually one being risqué. I tired of his conversation, sprinkled as it was with puns and *double entendres*. (French)

e.g. (EE JEE)
Abbreviation for *exempli gratia*, which means "for example." Some people think it stands for "example given"—if that helps you remember it, fine. E.g. is almost always abbreviated and written rather than spoken. Don't confuse it with the other itty-bitty Latin word i.e., which means "that is." (Latin)

en famille (anh fah·MEE)
At home; informally. (French)

et cetera (et CETT·uh·rah; et CETT·tra)
And so forth, and other things in the same class. Look carefully at the way it's spelled and do NOT say *eck* cetera. Do not abbreviate it *ect.* either. (Latin)

et tu, Brute? (ett TOO, BROO·tay)

Supposedly said by Julius Caesar when he saw his beloved friend Brutus among the conspirators about to kill him. We say it now when we feel betrayed by someone we've trusted—often just jokingly. If my friend agrees with my wife that I'm eating too much and gaining weight, I might say to him, *"Et tu, Brute?"* (Latin)

fiancé, fiancée (fee·ahn·SAY)

French. You know this one. Use the extra *e* when referring to a woman who is engaged to be married, fiancé if it's a man. (French)

folie à deux (foe·lee ah ·DEUH)

Craziness shared by two people. This is the name of a rare psychiatric disorder in which two people share a delusion or delusions. It's used in a more general way to describe any kind of weirdness two people share: The new house, which they designed together, is a *folie à deux*, loaded with the Victorian gingerbread they adore. (French)

grande dame (GRAN DAMM; GRANHD DAHM)

Literally, a great lady; a dignified, and/or aristocratic, and/or highly respected older woman. The expression may also refer to a woman who is or has been at the head of her field: She is the *grande dame* of romance novelists. (French)

hasta la vista (ah´·stah lah VEE·stah)

See you later; so long; goodbye. Arnold Schwarzenegger famously says in *Terminator 2: Judgment Day*, *"Hasta la vista*, baby" before blowing someone to smithereens. Never mind Arnold: This phrase is used as a lighthearted way to say goodbye. (Spanish)

honi soit qui mal y pense (aw·nee swah kee mal ee PAHNSS)

Shame to the person who thinks evil of it (that is, is suspicious of something or someone, or reads a bawdy message into it). Edward III of England supposedly said it after a woman's garter fell down at a ball: He put it on his own leg with these words. The Order of the Garter is the greatest honor that can be bestowed in the United Kingdom. (French)

hors de combat (ORE duh komm·BAH)

Out of commission, out of action, disabled. The head of our department has been *hors de combat* for two weeks because of illness. (French)

hors d'oeuvre (or DERV)

Most people know this means a little something before a meal, an appetizer, but many misspell it. Understandably. That combination of apostrophe and three vowels doesn't look like English, and it isn't. It's French and literally translates "outside of the work," or not part of the main course. Spell it correctly and be admired for your savvy.

i.e. (EYE EE)

Abbreviation for *id est*—that is, in other words. He told me he was leaving the company—*i.e.*, he had quit his job. Usually written rather than spoken, and almost always abbreviated i.e. Don't confuse this little word with e.g. (Latin)

in medias res (in MAY·dee·ahss RACE;
in MEE·dee·ahss RACE)

In the middle of things; in the middle of the action. We were sorting clothing for the rummage sale: John caught us in *medias res* and was annoyed that we were too busy to chat. (Latin)

infra dig (IN·frah DIG)

From *infra dignitatem*: beneath one's dignity. I consider fixing my own car *infra dig*. (Latin)

inshallah (in·shah ·LAH)

If Allah wills; God willing. A devout Muslim's conversation frequently includes this phrase. *Inshallah* I'll be able to afford to educate both children. (Arabic)

je ne sais quoi (zhuh nuh say KWAH)
Literally meaning "I don't know what." This phrase is useful in referring to any quality that is difficult to describe—a certain something. She isn't beautiful, but she has a *je ne sais quoi* that draws men to her. Even though the house is in disrepair, a certain *je ne said quoi* makes it attractive. (French)

Kinder, Kirche, Kuche (KIN·der, KEER·kuh, KOO·kuh)
Children, church, kitchen. A motto supposedly used by Kaiser Wilhelm II to describe a woman's lot in the 19th century. It became a part of Nazi propaganda under Adolph Hitler. It's used today to describe an antiquated female model: My husband believes in *Kinder, Kirche, and Kuche*, but I'm planning to be president of Hewlett-Packard. (German)

nota bene (NOE·tah BEH·neh)
Note well; take notice. Usually written and abbreviated NB, nota bene is a signal to pay particular attention to something particularly important. I might forward a letter with NBs in the margin to direct the reader's eyes to certain paragraphs. (Latin)

nuance (NOO·anhs; NYEW·anhs)
A subtle variation or distinction in meaning. Some of the *nuances* of Ingmar Bergman's films are lost on me. The adjective *nuanced* accordingly means marked by such fine shades of meaning: a *nuanced* performance of Handel's Water Music. (French)

que sera, sera; che sarà, sarà (kay sah·RAH, sah·RAH)
What will be, will be. Some of us remember Doris Day's famous solo in *The Man Who Knew Too Much* (spoiler alert): A couple's son is kidnapped while they are all vacationing in Morocco; she's convinced he's hidden in the house she's visiting and sings this favorite song, to which he responds. (Spanish or Italian, take your pick)

schadenfreude (SHAH·den·FROY·de)

Pleasure in someone else's misfortune. From German *Schaden*, meaning damage or harm, and *Freude*, joy. This is not an emotion anyone is proud of, but the experience is probably universal, so the word is a useful one. (German)

wunderkind (VOON·duhr·kinnd)

A child prodigy, someone remarkably talented in music or other field at an early age. Although the word literally means "wonder child," it may also be used of anyone who succeeds brilliantly at any age. (German)

zeitgeist (ZYTE·gyste; TZYTE·gyste)

Usually capitalized. The spirit of the times; the thoughts and feelings typical of a particular period of time. The *zeitgeist* of the 1960s encouraged young people to live for the moment. (German)

WordSet VI: Bibliophile Jean's Book Perusal Reveals Repressed Trauma

Jean was ready to leave the town library. A confirmed **bibliophile**, she loved to sit in the reading room's cushioned window-seat with a book by a favorite author. But today, for some reason, **perusal** of the shelves had **yielded** nothing that interested her. Then she noticed a book someone had left behind on a chair. It was *Moby-Dick*, by Herman Melville. Wondering why she'd never read it **hitherto**, she picked it up and took it to the window-seat.

SHE WASN'T THE KIND OF PERSON TO **RECOIL** FROM SIMPLE WORDS ON A PAGE. WHY ON EARTH HAD THAT **PECULIAR** BOOK AFFECTED HER SO STRANGELY?

She plunged immediately into the story of a 19th-century whaling ship out of Nantucket. She caught her breath as she read of the Pequod's **deranged** skipper, Captain Ahab, **obsessed** with finding the white whale that had bitten off his leg. As Jean read on, her heart began to beat uncomfortably fast. Her palms were moist, and her hands trembled. Why was the story frightening her? It was, as they say, only a story. Yet that was **indubitably** what was **transpiring**: She was becoming terrified by a work of fiction.

Suddenly, the room seemed to turn black as she nearly lost **consciousness**. She realized people were looking at her. **Abashed**, she hastily gathered her possessions and left the library for home. She couldn't **comprehend** her reaction. She wasn't the kind of person to **recoil** from simple words on a page. Why on earth had that **peculiar** book affected her so strangely?

Back in the small house she shared with Lucy, her **vivacious** 3-year-old beagle, Jean fixed herself a small supper. She didn't have much appetite; perhaps her **untoward** experience in the library had thrown her system out of **kilter**. Tired, she decided to turn in early.

It was not an easy night. She was troubled by horrible dreams in which she watched Captain Ahab lose his leg again and again to the giant white whale. She awoke the next morning, unrefreshed and **vexed** with herself. She needed to find a way to get over the effects of *Moby-Dick*. It might be the master work of an **illustrious** author, Herman Melville, but it had **engendered** nothing but trouble for her.

The dreams continued to **throng** her nights, destroying her rest. Exhausted, she **ultimately** sought the help of a therapist to **ameliorate** her situation. Hearing her story, the therapist **opined** that Jean might be a victim of **repressed** memory **syndrome**. Patiently, she worked with Jean to try to uncover the **trauma** lying in her past but **inaccessible** to her conscious mind. At last the memory surfaced: Jean and her father were swimming at the beach in Daytona Beach, Florida, when a shark had attacked her, seizing her by the ankle and dragging her out of her father's arms and under water. Incredibly, her father had saved her, beating and kicking at the big fish until it released its hold. The **ghastly** experience had probably lasted just seconds, but as she relived her terror she realized she'd never **endured** anything worse.

Jean **recollected** from the family photo album that they had stopped vacationing at Daytona Beach when she was just 5 years old. Her parents must have wanted to remove her from the place that might **revive** the memory of this **ordeal**. Not a word had ever been spoken about it; not an **iota** of evidence of any kind remained except a small scar around the back of her ankle. She'd always wondered what had caused it. Now she knew. And she also understood why the story of *Moby-Dick* had held such power over her.

thug (THUG) A criminal, especially a violent criminal. *Thug* sounds like a word coined on the streets of New York, but in fact it's Indian, from the Hindi word *thag*, a robber or criminal. The first thugs were members of a cult or fraternity that committed ritual murder to honor Kali, the Hindu goddess of destruction. By the 19th century they were evildoers without a religious motive roaming around India, strangling travelers and relieving them of their possessions. The crime was known as *Thuggee*.

Jean's Words, 1st Third

bibliophile (BIBB·lee·o·file´) A person who loves and/or collects books, from the Greek *philos*, loving, and *biblos*, book. Most librarians are bibliophiles, as are most people who, like Jean, haunt libraries. You don't hear the word all the time; it's fairly fancy.

perusal (peh·ROO·zul) Reading or examining carefully. Sasha claimed *perusal* of every word Tolstoy ever wrote. The verb is to peruse. Note the qualifier *carefully*, and don't use this word as a synonym for *look at*, as in "I *perused* the comics page." That sounds artificial, and it's inaccurate, not what we're striving for here.

yielded (YEEL·ded) In this context, to yield means to produce or give up. The library has failed to produce anything that interests Jean. The word is also used about crops: The meadow should *yield* 50 bushels of alfalfa. Yield can also mean give in or surrender: I *yielded* to a desire to go into the store.

hitherto (HIH·thur·too´, hih´·ther·TOO) Before; formerly; up until a certain time. *Hitherto* my friend, he dropped me when I became a goth. I have never *hitherto* visited Canada.

deranged (deh·RAYNJD) Insane; mentally disturbed; wandering in one's mind. The verb derange can take an object: Losing his leg *deranged* Ahab. Or one may simply be deranged: I realized my friend was *deranged* when he attacked me verbally again and again for no reason.

obsessed (ob·SESSD) Preoccupied with one idea. If I'm obsessed by photography, I live, think, and breathe photography. The word can carry a hint of pathology: Someone who's obsessed may be on the edge of mental illness. However, it's also used just to mean enormously interested in: She's *obsessed* with Facebook.

indubitably (in·DOO·bit·ub·lee, in·DYU·bit·ub·lee) Without a doubt; absolutely. *Indubitably*, she has decided to take a later plane. Brad Pitt is *indubitably* handsome. No doubt about it. The word is from the same root as *doubt*.

transpiring (tran·SPIRE·ing) The verb to transpire means to happen, to take place, or to develop. Has anything new *transpired* since I last saw you? A momentous event is *transpiring* even as we speak. My dictionary adds that it's used in "serious prose." It can give a nice little shine to yours.

consciousness (CON·shuss·ness) The state of being aware or awake. This is the state Jean returns to after nearly fainting. In a figurative sense, it can refer to one's awareness of almost anything: My *consciousness* of having worn the wrong clothes, her *consciousness* of Margot's dependence on her care, and so forth.

abashed (uh·BASHD) Embarrassed; ill at ease; off balance. I was *abashed* to learn that breakfast was not free, and Donald had paid for mine. To abash is to make someone else feel this way, though the past participle abashed is used much more often than any other form of the verb.

comprehend (komm´·prih·HEND) To understand or grasp. The word works for wider understanding than, well, understand. To comprehend means to get the whole thing: When Jason said his wife was ill, I *comprehended* why he had behaved so oddly. The word comes from the Latin root *prehendere*, which literally means to grasp; we get the word *prehensile*, able to grasp—like the elephant's *prehensile* trunk—from the same root.

✸ PRACTICING JEAN'S WORDS, 1ST THIRD

The words for the first third of Jean's story are:

abashed	deranged	obsessed
bibliophile	hitherto	perusal
comprehend	indubitably	transpiring
consciousness		yielded

A. Match the list words with their correct definitions in the right-hand column.

1. deranged   a. uncomfortable, ill at ease

2. abashed   b. gave in

3. yielded   c. preoccupied, narrowly focused on

4. obsessed   d. insane, wandering in mind

B. If I am a bibliophile, I _____.
    1. fear books   3. borrow books
    2. love books   4. publish Bibles

C. Fill in the blanks with the correct list words.
    1. When I tried to hold my breath for three minutes, I almost lost _____.
    2. I don't know what's wrong with Justin today: He's been so helpful _____.
    3. A careful _____ of her letter gave me no clue to her plans.
    4. I cannot _____ why anyone would dislike Rosie.
    5. Without subtitles, I couldn't tell what was _____ in the Israeli film.

D. Which list word is the closest antonym for *certainly not*?

E. Complete the following story with list words.

Though I'm no (book lover), I like my newspaper. But my (reading) of today's paper shocked me. Yesterday, police were forced to shoot a man who tried to kidnap a teenage girl. The (mentally ill) gunman (certainly) was able to (understand) what he was doing. However, he was so (preoccupied, fixated) with his beautiful victim it's unlikely he would have (surrendered) to the authorities. (Up till now) we haven't known such violence (happening) in our little town. Sadly, this will raise our (awareness) of the dangers that are out there.

Answers
A. 1. d; 2. a; 3. b; 4. c
B. b
C. 1. consciousness; 2. hitherto; 3. perusal; 4. comprehend; 5. transpiring
D. indubitably

E. bibliophile; perusal; deranged; indubitably; comprehend; obsessed; yielded; Hitherto; transpiring; consciousness

---

Please Don't Say That!

et cetera (et SETT·uh·ruh, et SETT·truh) This Latin phrase means and so forth, and others. I've written about it elsewhere, but the point's worth making twice. It's not *eck* cetera, and you must not pronounce it that way. I'm not trying to scare you, but it sounds illiterate.

Jean's Words, 2nd Third

recoil (rih·KOYL) To pull away or draw back because of something unwanted, ugly, or nasty: He *recoiled* in horror when he saw my kitchen. Jean doesn't see herself as someone who'd recoil, or flinch, at a spooky story. As you probably know, the prefix *re-* means back, again, or against. Recoil seems to include all three meanings.

peculiar (pih·KYUL·yer) Special or distinctive; strange; eccentric. Though the dictionary gives distinctive as the primary definition, in practice people use peculiar to mean strange or odd: What a *peculiar* way to dress for a safari! My aunt got *peculiar* as she aged: She kept her teeth in the freezer.

vivacious (vih·VAY·shuss, vye·VAY·shuss) Full of life and energy; lively. From the Latin *vivere*, to live. Lucy the beagle is probably good for Jean at this point, jumping around and taking her mistress's mind off her problems. My boss, a *vivacious* thirtyish business school graduate, keeps the whole department busy and productive.

untoward (un·TOE·ward, un·tuh·WARD) Unfavorable; difficult; unlucky; unfortunate. Whatever it is isn't happening at the right time or shouldn't have happened at all. We had an *untoward* incident with the alternator, and the car simply refused to move. Martha's trip to Seattle was *untoward*, as her son flew in to New York the same weekend to surprise her.

kilter (KILL·ter) Order or natural condition. If I'm off kilter, I'm not my usual self: I ate a bad grape or something. Mary's news that she was moving threw her boss, Jack, out of *kilter*. If something's off kilter, it's out of balance. Note that the expression can be either off kilter or out of kilter—your choice. No one knows the origin of this word.

vexed (VEXD) The verb is to vex. She vexes her teachers with her pranks. Vexed means annoyed, bothered, or even plagued. He was vexed during his run by horseflies buzzing round his head. A vexed question is a thorny or problematic one requiring much discussion. Compare with the noun *harassment*, page 73, which refers to more serious behavior.

illustrious (il·LUS·tree·us) Outstanding; famous for achievement. Melville is *illustrious* chiefly because of *Moby-Dick*, though he wrote *Typee*, *Billy Budd*, and several other works still read and admired. Contrast *notorious*, page 52, which means famous in a negative way, or infamous. Jesse James was a *notorious* bandit.

engendered (en·JEN·derd) The verb engender means to create or to bring forth. Used literally, it means to have offspring. It's usually used in a figurative way, meaning to generate or produce. The movie *The Birds engendered* an unreasonable fear of our feathered friends. Failure to understand another culture can engender prejudice. *Moby-Dick* has generated nothing but misery for Jean.

throng (THRONG) To crowd into: People *thronged* the new Nordstrom's. The dreams are crowding into Jean's mind as she tries to sleep. This verb can also mean to crowd in upon: The fans *thronged* media cupcake Paris Hilton when she arrived in Boston. The noun throng means a crowd.

ultimately (UHL·tih·muht·lee) Finally; in the end. *Ultimately*, the Greeks killed Hector and sacked and burned Troy. My plan to work all summer was *ultimately* a failure. Ultimate, meaning final, is a useful adjective: His *ultimate* decision was to leave the company.

ameliorate (uh·MEEL·yuh·rate´, uh·MEEL·ee·uh·rate´) To improve; to make better. I'm working to *ameliorate* the problem between my coworker and me. The antibiotic *ameliorated* the patient's condition immediately. My dictionary says the verb can be intransitive—that is, without an object: You can simply *ameliorate*, meaning grow better, but I've never seen or heard it used in that way.

✹ PRACTICING JEAN'S WORDS, 2ND THIRD

The words for the second third of Jean's story are:

ameliorate	peculiar	ultimately
engendered	recoil	untoward
illustrious	throng	vexed
kilter		vivacious

A. Choose the word that's the closest synonym for *ultimately*.

    1. very   3. finally

    2. impressively   4. untimely

B. Standing is to important as fame is to _____.

C. Fill in the blanks with the correct list words.

    1. When I entered the house, I could sense something was off _____.

    2. Lee seemed to _____ when I tried to take her hand.

    3. Tom's early visits to museums _____ in him a deep love of Egyptian culture.

    4. Tylenol and cold baths did nothing to _____ little Eliza's fever.

5. Weren't you _____ when Jim didn't show up?

D. If you are thronged, you are being _____.
  1. left alone 3. surrounded by people
  2. annoyed 4. beaten with a leather strap

E. Look at these three list adjectives:
  peculiar   vivacious   untoward
  1. Which one might apply to a popular high school cheerleader?
  2. Which one might you use to describe an odd or eccentric new acquaintance?
  3. Which one would apply to the best man's dropping the ring at the wedding?

F. Complete the following story with list words.

I was happy to see friends (crowd into) our house when we entertained John Connor, the (famous) author of *Kitty's Revenge*, and his (lively, energetic) wife, Rachel. One (unfortunate) occurrence (annoyed) me: An uninvited guest arrived and said John had stolen his plot! I saw John (draw back) as if he'd been hit. It was most (unusual, odd), as the heckler is no writer. (Finally) we got rid of him, but it threw us all off (our usual condition); to (make better, improve) our mood, we toasted our best-selling author with champagne.

Answers

A. 3

B. illustrious

C. 1. kilter; 2. recoil; 3. engendered; 4. ameliorate; 5. vexed

D. 3

E. 1. vivacious; 2. peculiar; 3. untoward

F. throng; illustrious; vivacious; untoward; vexed; recoil; peculiar; ultimately; kilter; ameliorate

Jean's Words, 3rd Third

opined (oe·PINED) To opine means to give or state as one's opinion: The therapist opined the reason for Jean's condition. Easy to remember, because you know what an opinion is (we all have them), and this is the verb form of opinion. The word is often used in reference to an expert's opinion: Dr. Lewis *opines* that the tumor is operable. The D.C. pundits *opine* that our candidate can win.

repressed (rih·PRESSD) Pushed beneath the surface, stifled. The verb to repress means to curb or to control. Unwanted thoughts or memories may be repressed. The military junta may repress a rebellion. Compare *suppressed*, page 183. Or Amos's maiden great-aunt may be *repressed* because she saw something nasty in the woodshed.

syndrome (SIN·drome) A collection of symptoms, as of a disease or condition. Some experts believe carpal tunnel *syndrome* is caused by computer work under improper conditions. Asperger's *syndrome* is characterized by, among other things, inability to grasp social cues.

trauma (TRAW·mah) From the Greek word for wound comes this word, meaning either a very bad physical injury or emotional experience, or the condition that occurs as a result of such events. She never recovered from the *trauma* of seeing her sister drown. *Trauma* as a result of the horrors of World War I was frequent. The participle *traumatized* describes a person who has endured such an event. The adjective *traumatic* is useful, but please reserve it for describing a seriously stressful experience: Don't say it was *traumatic* to miss lunch.

inaccessible (in′·ack·SESS·ih·bl) Incapable of being reached, literally or figuratively: He put the suitcases in the attic, where they're basically *inaccessible*. Her mother was cold and emotionally *inaccessible*. You can also call a book that's difficult to understand, or a city in Mexico that's hard to reach, inaccessible.

ghastly (GAST·lee) Frightening or terrifying; unpleasant or disagreeable. In the first sense: The *ghastly* phantom beckoned to Scrooge. In the second sense: Let's not go to that *ghastly* party again this year. Jean's experience was ghastly in the first: frightening in the extreme.

endured (en·DYOORED, en-DOORED) To endure means to suffer or to go through: She *endured* great pain when she had a root canal. That's the way it's used here. It also means to tolerate or put up with: I couldn't *endure* the endless sawing and hammering. And it means to last or continue: The noise *endured* the entire night. These mountains have *endured* for centuries.

recollected (reh´·kuh·LEK·ted) Remembered. When you recollect, you cast your mind back to a past time to retrieve its memories. You can recollect a specific something—a New Year's Eve party in 1995, for instance—or you can simply sit back and recollect: As I *recollect*, it was about midmorning when he appeared.

revive (rih·VIVE) Literally, to return to consciousness; to breathe new life into: The lifeguard *revived* the unconscious swimmer. To restore; to bring back: John's photographs *revived* my interest in kite surfing. To cause to flourish: All that watering has *revived* the roses. Without an object, to come to life: After a long drink of ice water, I began to *revive*.

ordeal (or·DEEL) A difficult or painful experience undergone, certainly what the young Jean underwent. In ancient times, an ordeal was a sort of test to prove your character or worth: The Greek gods and goddesses were constantly subjecting mortals to various ordeals, and in 17th-century New England people accused of witchcraft were dunked in water as a means to prove their guilt or innocence. It still has that flavor of severely testing a person, sometimes over a period of time, unlike trauma, earlier in this list.

iota (eye·OE·tah) The very tiniest bit. We get *jot* (as in "not a jot of truth to that rumor") from the same root: In Latin, *i*'s are always turning into *j*'s. There wasn't one *iota* of mud on my nice clean floor. Nor is there even the smallest piece of evidence of the shark attack except the scar on Jean's leg. Compare *scintilla*, page 120. Both are useful to know.

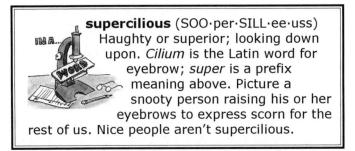

supercilious (SOO·per·SILL·ee·uss) Haughty or superior; looking down upon. *Cilium* is the Latin word for eyebrow; *super* is a prefix meaning above. Picture a snooty person raising his or her eyebrows to express scorn for the rest of us. Nice people aren't supercilious.

✹ PRACTICING JEAN'S WORDS, 3RD THIRD

The words for the last third of Jean's story are:

endured	opined	repressed
ghastly	ordeal	revive
inaccessible	recollected	syndrome
iota		trauma

A. Match the list words with their correct definitions in the right-hand column:

1. endured   a. remembered
2. opined   b. stated
3. recollected   c. suffered
4. repressed   d. stifled

B. Which two list words are close, if not exact, synonyms?

C. Fill in the blanks with the correct list words.

1. This article contains not one _____ of original writing.

2. Someone should tell Nella to pitch that _____ dress off the fire escape.

3. Raynaud's _____ causes the fingers to lose circulation and turn yellow.

4. Don't visit: She lives in that _____ location so she won't have to see anyone.

D. Which list word is the closest antonym for *knock out*?

E. Complete the following story with list words.

The (painful test) of coming into a room full of strangers is one we've all (lived through), but that doesn't make it less (horrible, unpleasant). I recently (remembered) being the new girl in school: I (held back) nervous hiccups all through breakfast. Tenney Middle School was in the most (hard to reach) part of town, and my father got lost driving me, which didn't help. He tried to (restore) my spirits by telling jokes, then (stated as his belief) that I was a chicken without one (tiny bit) of guts. Neither of these stratagems worked. For a child, facing that sea of unfamiliar faces is close to a (dreadful emotional experience). I was comfortable at Tenney after a few days, but the memory of that morning is still painful.

Answers

A. 1. c; 2. b; 3. a; 4. d

B. ordeal, trauma

C. 1. iota; 2. ghastly; 3. syndrome; 4. inaccessible

D. revive

E. ordeal; endured; ghastly; recollected; repressed; inaccessible; revive; opined; iota; trauma

Superlative Synonyms for So-So Syllables

We all have words we depend on too much. Our culture tends to overwork words; because everyone knows what they mean, it's easier just to keep using them than to try for a newer, simpler, or brighter synonym. There are three categories of words that I'm going to ask you to avoid whenever possible.

First, here's a list of words that are simply worn out from overuse. People are tired of hearing them. I've provided you with some suggested equivalents, and I suggest you avoid the weary ones and consider the sprightly ones when you write or speak.

boring   *Tedious* is a lovely synonym for the overexposed *boring*. It has a suggestion of lengthiness.

Donna's account of her recovery from a broken toe is detailed and *tedious*.

Monotonous is derived from the words for *one* and *tone* and, accordingly, means boring from lack of variety.

The speaker's voice was *monotonous*, as if she was hard of hearing, and I became increasingly sleepy as the speech progressed.

✳

broke   If you are out of money, you are *destitute*, *insolvent*, and *impoverished*. Note that these are serious words, not meant for a situation that will resolve itself by Monday. *Short of cash* would cover that.

✳

funny   If it's super-funny, try *hilarious*. If it tickles you
          and makes you feel a little superior, how about
          amusing, entertaining, or *humorous*? If it makes
          you laugh in part because it's ridiculous (like the
          guy with lampshade on head), the word you want
          may be *comical*. Is it clever? Consider *witty*. If it's
          absurd, foolish, even odd, *ludicrous* is a wonderful
          word.

The spectacle of George Clooney dressed as a
ballerina is *ludicrous*.

You may be laughing not with them, but at them. For a good
synonym with a shot of scorn, I suggest *risible* (RIZZ·ih·bl)
or *derisory* (duh·RYE·zuh·ree). Note that both can mean either provoking laughter or laughing in a scornful way.

She felt his attempt to act sophisticated at the cast
party was *risible*.

Her *derisory* remarks clearly hurt the boy, who was
trying hard to impress her.

✳

great   Everyone overuses this one. And some of my
          synonyms are themselves overused: *excellent,
          fantastic, fabulous, sensational, super, terrific.* Just pick
          one that you yourself at least haven't been
          overworking. And remember that sometimes a
          simple *good* or *fine* can be more effective than these
          hyperbolic (exaggerated) words.

✳

gross   This word has been overused since even I was in
          college. If you don't like the new building, perhaps
          it's just *unattractive*. If it's a very bad dinner, maybe
          you could try *repulsive, revolting,* or *disgusting*. In
          the same family are *repugnant* and *repellent*: The
          objects of these adjectives almost physically push

you away by their awfulness. I personally like *vile*, which has a suggestion of immorality. The five-dollar synonym is *rebarbative*, which comes from the word for beard and means irritating in the extreme.

✳

in love   You're *enamoured* if you're fascinated by the object of your affection. Note that you say enamoured *of*. You can be *crazy about*; you can be *mad for*. You may be *amorous* or *ardent* in showing your feelings toward this person, or even *passionate*.

Dana was thrilled by Travis's *passionate* words to her in the summer house.

✳

love   We all use this one too much. Even the mailman says he loves me. *Affection* is a good word that can be used for fondness for anyone from one's two-year-old niece to one's spouse of 50 years. It tends to be habitual and steady. *Devotion* is also steady and habitual, but deeper than affection. *Fondness* suggests tenderness and perhaps a certain blindness to faults. *Adoration*? Pretty intense, and tends to put the adorer in the down position looking up; use with care. *Passion* connotes a tendency toward the physical.

✳

nice   That's a pretty tired word to use for people. How is the person nice? Open and well-intentioned? Try *pleasant*, *kind*, *sweet*, or *warm-hearted*. Generous? How about *munificent* or *charitable* if it's to do with sharing money or resources? Thoughtful? *Solicitous* is good if the person is truly concerned about another's welfare. All-around the best? *Lovely*.

*

out of it   I'm happy to share quite a few fresh synonyms for *out of it* or *just not getting it*—fresher than the overworked *out to lunch*, anyway. You can say a person is *oblivious*. Note that the adjective takes the preposition *to* or *of*.

She was *oblivious* to the shrieking in the next room.

Oblivious of his friend's distress, he happily continued his story.

A friend of mine refers to drivers who sit between two lanes, drive 25 miles per hour in every circumstance, and turn without signaling as *blivits*, as in "I've got to find a way around this blivit." You may also call a person *insensible*.

I believe Ernest is utterly *insensible* of the damage he has done.

Be aware that this word can also mean insensitive. *Obtuse* is another synonym, but it indicates the poor guy is chronically stupid and can't help it.

*

smile, verb   *To beam* is a nice, warm synonym. Nice people beam. If you *grin*, you're really showing teeth. If you *smirk*, on the other hand, you may not show your teeth at all, and you're more pleased with yourself than with anything else. People who smirk are not generally feeling friendly, although they may be feeling smug. *Grin* and *smirk* are nouns you can substitute for the noun *smile* as well.

*

tired   Maybe you're just a little tired: You could be *fatigued*. Or if you're really tired, you're *all in*, or *exhausted*, or *wiped out*, or, informally, *pooped*. No doubt you're pooped after reading all this.

*

Second, a word may become overused because people believe they sound impressive when they include it in conversation or e-mail. The truth is that there is little reason to prefer the overused, stuffy words in the left-hand column to the simple, clear words on the right:

Stuffy Word		Plain English Synonym
delimitations	↔	limits
facilitate	↔	aid
impact (verb)	↔	affect
incentivize	↔	motivate, inspire
paradigm	↔	model, example
parameters	↔	limits, factors
utilize	↔	use

I'm not suggesting you stop using new vocabulary words, or long words, but I am proposing that you ask yourself whether you're really adding to meaning or simply adding to length and complexity. In particular, don't string chains of long words together.

The audibility degradation factor occasioned by the blasting activity was within the delimitations of an operant disincentive.

You practically need a translator to tell you that nobody wanted to work because the blasting was so noisy.

Third, some words were coined to apply to a number of situations. They are what I call covering words, because they cover a multitude of possibilities and as such can be quite valuable. An *event*, for example, describes any number of happenings, from a birthday party to a funeral, which makes it useful word. However—and it's a big however—don't think that you sound more important or businesslike if you use the word *event* in place of something specific, such as a Mother's Day brunch. You actually sound pompous and possibly obscure. Use specific language whenever possible. It's a favor to your readers and listeners. The words on the left apply to general situations, and they are overworked; give them a rest by using such specific language as I've provided on the right whenever you can.

Covering Language		Concrete Language
affair	↔	party, benefit, concert
contact (verb)	↔	e-mail, telephone, visit
event	↔	dance, picnic, gallery opening
facility	↔	house, office building, barn
precipitation	↔	rain, snow, sleet, hail
relationship	↔	friendship, marriage, partnership
situation	↔	job change, illness, misunderstanding

Of course you can't always substitute specific language, which is why the covering words are often appropriate. I'm just asking you to be specific when you can. You'll create a much more memorable impression that way.

Bottom line: Avoid tired language; don't use a stuffy, complex word when a simple one will do; and use concrete language whenever possible.

WordSet VII: Thunderstruck and Vulnerable, Robert Seeks to Surmount Loss

Robert put his hands in his pockets and blew a low whistle. A careful **scrutiny** of the empty street **revealed** that there was still no Michelle. She was already 20 minutes late. It wasn't like her. He **lounged** against the **substantial** bulk of the local bank and tapped a foot. Still no Michelle. The sound of running feet caused him to spin around. **Giddy** with relief, he caught her in his arms and kissed her **ardently**. In his **exhilaration**, he failed to **perceive** that his show of affection was returned only **tepidly**. At any rate, his joy was **transient**. It was easy to see something was **amiss**. Michelle's eyes wouldn't meet his, and her **countenance** was grave.

ROBERT BECAME INCREASINGLY **APPREHENSIVE**
HE WAS EXTREMELY **VULNERABLE** IN RELATIONSHIPS

"What is it, Michelle? What's going on?" he asked. Instead of answering, she took his hand and led him to a park bench across the street. They sat silent for a moment or two; Robert became increasingly **apprehensive**. **Impervious** to the hurdles he faced at work, and **invincible** in sports—basketball, tennis, whatever—he was extremely **vulnerable** in relationships.

"Robert, I can't see you again." The words caught him like a stone thrown at his chest. "We aren't right for each other. Please"—as he moved closer to her, her hands came up as if to **avert** a blow—don't make it worse by asking questions."

Painfully, Robert made his way home. Everything in his little apartment reminded him of Michelle. How was he expected to **surmount** such heartbreak? Yesterday, she'd been warm, loving, his girl. Today it was over. There was no making sense of it.

Despondently, he opened a can of soup. Even if your world **imploded**, you still had to eat. The **eerie** part was that he sensed strongly that Michelle still cared. She hadn't been entirely able to hide the regret, the **remorse**, he'd felt behind her brief speech. Then why? Why?

His cell phone rang. Michelle! he responded **reflexively**. But of course it wasn't. Marcus wanted to know if he'd come down for pickup basketball in half an hour. Listlessly, Robert agreed: Maybe a **cardiovascular** workout would help relieve the blues he was **contending** with. He joined his buddies in the park and played one on one for an hour, then headed back home.

"Dearest Michelle," he e-mailed her. "I respect your decision, but I feel you owe me an explanation. Please respond. I love you." The message tumbled into the **void** of **cyberspace**. He heard nothing for three days. Then one morning his inbox lit up with her name! He read: "Robert, you're right. Your kindness to me **merits** some explanation of my actions. Will you meet me at Colleen's after work?"

Somehow Robert got through his work day and, his heart hammering, made it to the restaurant that was one of their favorites. She had arrived before him and was seated in a booth at the back. He **negotiated** a path to her through the crowd watching a baseball game on TV.

"Listen to me, Robert, because I'm not going to **reiterate** this story." Michelle spoke rapidly. "You know I was adopted as an infant. Since you and I were getting serious, I felt I needed to learn what I could about my birth parents. I was able to meet my grandmother and, to my **consternation**, discovered my mother has been in and out of prison for years." She paused, as if to **gauge** his reaction. "Aren't you going to say anything, Robert?" Her eyes filled with tears that she brushed away almost angrily.

Robert was **thunderstruck**. "What do you want me to say? That I give a darn what a woman you've never met has done? That I think it makes a particle of difference? I cannot believe you'd pull us apart over something so meaningless."

"Robert, I have her genes. She's a **felon**, Robert: a career criminal. Would you want to live with me? Would you want to have children with me?"

Robert smiled a slow smile. "Michelle, I'm taking that as a proposal, and I accept. Your mother could be a second-story man for all I care. We're going to be married, and we're going to live happily ever after." And they did.

Robert's Words, 1st Third

scrutiny (SKROO·tin·ee) Careful inspection or examination; surveying. Robert is eyeballing the street intensely because he's nervous about Michelle's lateness. Paul's behavior regarding the disposition of his parents' estate doesn't bear *scrutiny*. The verb scrutinize means to inspect carefully: I *scrutinized* the contract for any possible loophole.

revealed (ree·VEELD) To reveal something is to show it or make it known. I might reveal a secret I've kept for years. If your friends have been asking where you go every weekend, you might reveal the answer: You've taken up ballroom dancing. She *revealed* her inmost longings to her best friend.

lounged (LOWNJD) The verb to lounge means to behave comfortably or in a relaxed, often lazy, manner. I *lounge* around the house on Saturday mornings. Robert is leaning (more or less comfortably) against the wall of a building.

substantial (sub·STAN·shull) Well built; solid: Robert can lean against that building and it's not going to fall over. It can also mean considerable: Her husband died and left a *substantial* fortune. He left her enough to keep her comfortable and then some. Margery had put on a *substantial* amount of weight.

giddy (GID·ee) Dizzy; silly; sometimes confused. Take the Tilt-A-Whirl ride at the carnival and you may become giddy from being tossed around. If I learn a fabulous piece of news, I may become giddy with joy. Hiram was *giddy* from listening to their rapid-fire conversation. It's a lighthearted word, likely to be used for happy rather than sad experiences.

ardently (AR·dent·lee) With much feeling; passionately. It's the opposite of half-heartedly, because one's whole heart is involved. You can be ardently supportive of a presidential candidate. You can ardently work for prison reform. You can, as Robert does, kiss someone ardently. A useful word.

exhilaration (egg·zill´·uh·RAY·shun) A state of excitement and happiness. The team's victory was greeted with *exhilaration*. The verb, naturally, means to overjoy or excite: You might be exhilarated to learn you got the job. I think of it as a sort of fizzy state, giving off champagne bubbles.

perceive (purr·SEEVE) To notice; to be aware of; to see. I *perceive* that Jason is ill. The principal *perceived* that the sixth-grader was truly sorry for biting his classmate. If something is perceived, it may not actually be so, but it's regarded that way: Betty was *perceived* as a snob; she was actually just very shy.

tepidly (TEH·pid·lee) Not wholeheartedly (see *ardently* on page 158); in a lukewarm fashion. The adjective tepid has the literal meaning of lukewarm: You give a baby tepid baths so you don't risk burning the poor little thing. No one wants to be kissed tepidly.

transient (TRAN-zee·unt, TRAN·zhunt [There are a lot of ways to pronounce this word; I chose the two I hear most frequently.]) Not lasting; passing quickly. Washington, D.C., has a *transient* population because of military postings and politicians coming and going. Morning mist on the lake is *transient*. Robert's joy passes quickly out of existence.

amiss (uh·MISS) Not right; gone wrong; wrongly. The word can be either an adjective or an adverb—that is, something may *be* amiss (adjective), or it may *go* amiss (adverb). When I saw the body on the floor, I knew something was *amiss*. Our plans had definitely gone *amiss*. What's *amiss* with Cynthia?

countenance (KOWN·tuh·nunss) Face; expression. One's countenance may be indicative of one's mood, or people may try to read one's mood from one's countenance. Her calm *countenance* hid her terror of public speaking. I almost laughed at his woeful *countenance* when he learned he'd received only an A-.

✳ PRACTICING ROBERT'S WORDS, 1ST THIRD

The words for the first third of Robert's story are:

amiss	giddy	scrutiny
ardently	lounged	substantial
countenance	perceive	tepidly
exhilaration	revealed	transient

A. Fill in the blanks with the correct list words.

1. He looked at me hard; knowing the sin I'd committed, I couldn't bear his_____.

2. Keith, realizing he'd won the Iron Man Triathlon, was filled with _____.

3. She came home late and found her husband waiting with an angry _____.

4. Ken _____ around the apartment till 2:00 in the afternoon, doing nothing.

5. Her sweet smile _____ nothing of her inner feelings.

B. Which two list adverbs (adverbs tell how something is done) are close, if not exact, antonyms?

C. Match the list words with their correct definitions in the right-hand column.

1. giddy   a. wrong

2. transient   b. solid

3. substantial   c. not lasting

4. amiss   d. dizzy

D. Which sentence uses the word *perceive* correctly?

1. Danae failed to perceive that Justin was really hurt by her leaving the job.

2. On your 21st birthday you are likely to perceive more gifts than usual.

3. I don't perceive anyone to miss more than two lessons during the semester.

4. Did Tom ever perceive the money you took from his wallet?

E. Complete the following story with list words.

One Saturday morning as I (hung out comfortably) in bed, the phone rang. "You've won $50,000 in the Digest Sweepstakes! Congratulations! That's a (considerable) sum," said a voice. "Right," I answered (in a lukewarm fashion). "And pigs fly." "No, this is for real," said my caller (passionately). Someone will call with a check. Give it your

(close inspection): You'll see nothing's (incorrect, wrong)."
What if it's true? I thought in excitement; but my joy was
(not lasting). It had to be phony. Then the doorbell rang.
A man with a cheerful (expression) stood outside. "It's true!"
he cried. "You've won!" He waved the promised check.
(Silly) with (excitement), I began to (see) my luck had
turned.

Answers
A. 1. scrutiny; 2. exhilaration; 3. countenance; 4. lounged;
   5. revealed
B. ardently, tepidly
C. 1. d; 2. c; 3. b; 4. a
D. 1
E. lounged; substantial; tepidly; ardently; scrutiny; amiss;
   transient; countenance; giddy; exhilaration; perceive

Robert's Words, 2nd Third

apprehensive (app´·pree·HEN·siv) Nervous; concerned;
   expecting something bad to happen. Some animals become
   apprehensive ahead of an earthquake. Karen said her parents
   would be glad to see us, but it was 3 a.m. and I was
   apprehensive. Many people are *apprehensive* about taking a
   driver's test.

impervious (im·PURR·vee·uss) Not able to be hurt, damaged,
   or penetrated. If you're emotionally tough, you may be
   impervious to insults; your sofa, treated with Scotch-Gard,
   may be impervious to the red wine spilled on it; and your
   jacket may be impervious to the wind.

invincible (in·VIN·sih·bl) Unable to be defeated. In other
   words, Robert always wins—at least in sports. The word
   comes from the same root as vanquish, meaning to conquer
   or defeat. Helen Reddy sings, "I am strong, I am *invincible*,
   I am woman." You don't mess with someone invincible.

vulnerable (VUHL·ner·a·bl) The opposite of impervious, vulnerable means able to be wounded physically or emotionally, having a chink in one's armor: She was *vulnerable* to jokes about her height. Open to being hurt or damaged: A boat that spends the winter uncovered is *vulnerable* to damage by rain and snow. Open; unguarded: The fort was *vulnerable* to attack. Robert is easily hurt in the area of romantic relationships.

avert (uh·VERT) To ward off; to avoid. If I take the turnpike, I may avert a huge traffic jam. Avert can also mean to turn away: *Avert* your eyes when the surgery begins. Michelle raises her hands as if to protect herself from being hit.

surmount (surr·MOWNT) To rise above; to overcome. Often used with the object *obstacle*, as in "I *surmounted* every obstacle in my path to the presidency." Robert fears he won't be able to rise above his heartbreak. *Sur* is a Latin prefix meaning over, above.

despondently (des·PON·dent·lee) Sadly; hopelessly; in a depressed or dejected manner. The adjective is despondent: If I'm despondent, I'm in the dumps, feeling low and miserable. The word is not as strong as despairing, but it's getting there.

imploded (im·PLOE·ded) To implode means to collapse or burst in on itself, like an explosion turned inward. Robert's world has collapsed in upon itself. Figuratively, the word can mean to self-destruct: A ring of organized crime might implode from corruption and betrayal within. My sand castle *imploded* from the weight of all the seashells I added.

eerie (EER·ee) Weird; odd; strange enough to give you the creeps. A useful Halloween word: Ghosts and ghouls are eerie. You can have an eerie feeling that someone is following you. Holly had an *eerie* resemblance to her dead sister.

remorse (re·MORSS) Regret laced with feelings of guilt for some act committed. Remorse is a strong emotion; the root word means *to bite*. If I'm experiencing remorse, I'm wishing I could undo an ugly deed or at least make amends. Robert senses that Michelle isn't happy with her decision: She feels bad about it.

reflexively (rih·FLEK·siv·lee) In an automatic or unthinking manner, the way a reflex works: The doctor hits your knee with a little hammer and your leg swings out *reflexively*. It can refer to an ingrained practice or habit: People in the Secret Service *reflexively* knock down and surround the president when they hear a gunshot. Robert is so used to receiving calls from Michelle that, when his phone rings, he automatically thinks it's she.

✹ PRACTICING ROBERT'S WORDS, 2ND THIRD

The words for the second third of Robert's story are:

apprehensive	impervious	reflexively
avert	imploded	remorse
despondently	invincible	surmount
eerie		vulnerable

A. Which list word is the closest antonym for *impervious*?

B. Match the list words with their correct definitions in the right-hand column.

1. despondently   a. worried, nervous

2. apprehensive   b. automatically

3. invincible   c. in despair, hopelessly

4. reflexively   d. undefeatable

C. Fill in the blanks with the correct list words.

1. Dad couldn't _____ the blow of losing the farm and became deeply depressed.

2. Eons ago, some of those stars _____ on themselves and disappeared.

3. I'd been unkind to Jesse when she was alive; now I was ashamed and filled with _____.

4. The only way to _____ a huge fine is to give the IRS what it wants immediately.

D. Which list word describes a scary novel full of ghosts?

E. Complete the following story with list words.

Julia sat (gloomily, hopelessly) on her front steps. How could she (avoid) a meeting with Harold? Her heart, once (unable to be penetrated), was now so (easily wounded). She was (nervous), fearing she might burst into tears. It was (weird) how quickly she'd fallen in love with him. Now he was marrying Elsa. Hateful Elsa, she thought (automatically). When she'd heard the news, it was as if her formerly (unable to be defeated) heart had (collapsed in upon itself). If I'd been more fun to be with, she thought with (regret), Harold might be marrying me. But that wasn't who she was. Now here came Harold. She'd just have to (overcome) her feelings and put on a good show.

Answers

A. vulnerable

B. 1. c; 2. a; 3. d; 4. b

C. 1. surmount; 2. imploded; 3. remorse; 4. avert

D. eerie

E. despondently; avert; impervious; vulnerable; apprehensive; eerie; reflexively; invincible; imploded; remorse; surmount

Robert's Words, 3rd Third

cardiovascular ((kar´·dee·oe·VASS·kyuh·lurr) Of or involving the heart and the blood vessels. Also, and this is the way it's used in this story, designed to cause a temporary increase in the heart rate: *cardiovascular* exercise. Exercise makes most things better, right? Gets those painkilling endorphins into your blood stream. Exercise strenuously for half an hour three times weekly to get the *cardiovascular* benefits that help keep you healthy.

contending (kun·TEN·ding) To contend means to do battle; to fight; to strive in an argument; to dispute. Robert's struggling with the blues. If I contend with the power company over my bill, I disagree and am ready to argue the issue. Contend can also mean to compete: My sister and I *contended* for our parents' attention.

void (VOYD) One dictionary offers me 18 meanings for void. Primarily, and as used here, it means a large, hollow space. It can mean a lack that's felt as deprivation: Her resignation leaves a huge *void* in our division. The adjective void means empty, vacant; also, lacking or devoid. His work was *void* of meaning now that Maura was gone. Its legal usage means ineffective, or not in force: The contract is null and *void*.

cyberspace (SYE·ber·SPAYSS) The space where computer transactions occur. The electronic medium of computer networks, where online communication takes place. It can refer to an imaginary realm; for example, the landscape of a computer game exists in cyberspace. Like the sock that vanishes in the dryer but is alive and well in some parallel universe, e-mail messages sometimes seem to disappear into cyberspace.

merits (MEH·rits) To merit means to deserve or earn. Michelle feels Robert deserves an explanation because he has been good to her. You can use it just as you would the word deserve: John deserves a reward; he *merits* one. The noun merit means worth, value, superior quality, excellence: The novel was utterly without *merit*; Kelly received a *merit* scholarship.

negotiated (nuh·GOE·she·ate´·ed) The verb to negotiate means to bargain or discuss terms; to arrange or settle: Stacy *negotiated* a good divorce settlement for Jim. It also means to pass around or through successfully: He *negotiated* the falls in his kayak. That's the meaning here: Robert manages to get through the crowded room. Note that none of my dictionaries gives the newscaster pronunciation nuh·GOE·see·ate·ed. Don't you dare say that.

reiterate (re·IH·tuh·rayt´) To say again; to repeat. To say, do, or perform again, sometimes excessively, or too much: She *reiterated* her demands until we finally gave in. He *reiterated* the procedure until everyone understood how to do it. Note that if you reiterate twice, you have said or done it THREE times.

consternation (kon´·stur·NAY·shun) Confusion; amazement; dismay. If I experience consternation, I'm puzzled and more than a bit upset. Michelle is amazed and horrified at her discovery. To my *consternation*, I discovered I had forgotten the tickets. The Latin root *sternere* means to throw down—in consternation, one is figuratively thrown.

gauge (GAYJE) It's not pronounced GAWJE, despite the spelling. To measure or determine the dimensions; to estimate or judge. I may try to *gauge* the distance from my back door to the bird feeder. Michelle is trying to figure out how Robert is reacting to her news. A gauge is, of course, whatever you use to measure or estimate: a pressure *gauge* for tires, for example.

thunderstruck (THUN·der·struck´) A handy word meaning knocked sideways. If I'm thunderstruck, I'm stunned; I'm filled with amazement, even consternation. I may be thunderstruck by either good or bad news: I was *thunderstruck* to hear Ellie had passed chemistry. Robert is thunderstruck, not by the significance of Michelle's news, but by its triviality in his eyes.

felon (FELL·un) A criminal; one who's committed and/or been convicted of a crime. The *felon* will be tried in the Cincinnati courts by a jury of his peers. A felony is a crime that's more serious than a misdemeanor: murder or arson, for example, rather than speeding or running a red light. Astonishingly, a felon is also an infection around the nail of a finger or toe.

✹ PRACTICING ROBERT'S WORDS, 3RD THIRD

The words for the last third of Robert's story are:

cardiovascular	felon	negotiated
consternation	gauge	reiterate
contending	merits	thunderstruck
cyberspace	void	

A. Salary is to worker as jail time is to _____.

B. Fill in the blanks with the correct list words.

1. After Donnie went off to college, I felt a great _____ in my life.

2. She was filled with _____ when she received the disturbing letter.

3. The sailboat neatly _____ the narrow channel into the harbor.

4. Use your computer to play games, find a job, or meet your mate in _____.

5. He said nothing about the sale of the house, so it was hard to _____ his feelings.

C. Choose the word that's the closest synonym for *contending*.

1. annoying   3. competing

2. being happy   4. caring for

D. Match the list words with their correct definitions in the right-hand column.

1. cardiovascular	a. say or do again
2. thunderstruck	b. deserves
3. gauge	c. of the heart and lungs
4. reiterate	d. measure
5. merits	e. astounded

E. Complete the following story with list words.

Barry was (amazed) when Mary told him she'd (arranged) a contract with a rival firm. "How could you?" he began to (repeat) again and again. "We've (competed) with Ace Can for years. Don't you feel like a (criminal) going over to their side?" "No," said Mary, "But your (dismay) (deserves) an explanation. The other night I was gaming in (the electronic medium of computer networks) and after winning Warquest a dozen times, I realized I'm smart. You won't promote me or give me a raise. My work life was a (vacant, empty space). So I applied at Ace and they took me." She paused to (assess) his reaction and realized he was weeping.

Answers

A. felon

B. 1. void; 2. consternation; 3. negotiated; 4. cyberspace; 5. gauge

C. 3

D. 1. c; 2. e; 3. d; 4. a; 5. b

E. thunderstruck; negotiated; reiterate; contended; felon; consternation; merits; cyberspace; void; gauge

14

Bad or Nonexistent Words: Avoid Them at All Costs

This chapter lists words that you must avoid! It's a teeny chapter, but it just may be the most important one in the book. You can hardly do worse than write or say a word that is hideously ungrammatical or doesn't even exist. When you do, people think you are dumb or poorly educated. You're not reading this book so people will think that.

On page 170 I've listed the most common of these words, which I myself would never use. Note that you can find some of them in some dictionaries, where they're described as dialect, or informal, or variants. When a dictionary labels a word that way, the red flag should go up. I suggest you leave them strictly alone.

Please Don't Say That!
processes (PROH·sess·ez) This familiar word has, over the last decade or so, been saddled with a decidedly *un*familiar plural. People who should know better are saying PROH·sess·eez, apparently based on a specious analogy to words that end in *–is*, such as basis, emphasis, and oasis, which form plurals by substituting –es for –is. Hello! Process does *not* end in *–is*. If you're doing this, for heaven's sake stop it.

Bad or Nonexistent Word		Correct Word
ain't	↔	aren't, isn't
alot	↔	a lot
alright	↔	all right
anyways	↔	anyway
goodby	↔	goodbye
heighth	↔	height
irregardless	↔	regardless
marshall	↔	marshal (as in *marshal the troops*)
momento	↔	memento (same root as memory)
nother	↔	in the phrase *a whole nother*; use *another whole*
regards	↔	in the phrase *in regards to*; it's *in regard to*
renumerative	↔	remunerative
restauranteur	↔	restaurateur
revelant	↔	relevant (same with irrevelant)
somewheres	↔	somewhere (same with all the -*wheres*)

15

WordSet VIII: Massive Dissonance Prompts Daphne to Persevere Undeterred

For the third time that evening, Daphne tapped on the door of Gwen's room. "I'm really sorry, Gwen, but I'm trying to sleep. Got a big day tomorrow. Could you keep it down?" The metallic **dissonance** of ACDC crashed and thumped throughout the apartment, and Daphne was developing a **massive** headache. Whenever she mentioned headphones, Gwen agreed with **alacrity**—but never got around to using them. It was **infuriating**.

For the hundredth time she wished her **mundane** job as a bookstore cashier paid enough to **enable** her to afford this tiny apartment on her own. Privacy was **illusory**, and the construction so cheap you could hear a pin drop two rooms away. **Reflecting** on her situation, Daphne admitted to herself **ruefully** that she alone was to blame. She'd **impulsively** asked Gwen, only a **casual** friend, to share the apartment when her roommate, Sheri (of blessed memory), had left to get married. She should, Daphne now perceived, have inquired closely about Gwen's musical **predilections**. A blast from ACDC shook the room. Too late now.

Or not. Tomorrow actually was a big day. She had an interview with a small but **reputable** publisher of high-quality art books. The online ad read, "Sales Rep. Respectable salary plus generous **commission**." She had loved studying art and photography in school. The job had **distinct** possibilities, Daphne thought, including the **ineffable** pleasure of telling

Gwen—politely, of course—to **initiate** her search for a new residence.

Morning dawned drizzly. Cheered by her hope of **attaining** the twin goals of employment and silence, she **trudged** the four blocks to the subway.

A half hour later, she entered a gleaming new brick-and-marble **edifice** and the elevator, **ascending** the 15 floors to Grainger's offices. The receptionist smiled. "I'll tell Scott you're here."

"Daphne Koleva?" She turned to face a short, smiling, **auburn**-haired man. "I'm Scott Harper, head of human resources. In fact, *most* of human resources. Welcome to Grainger Publishing."

Despite Scott's friendly manner, the interview proved **intimidating**. His questions **relative** to painting and photography revealed her knowledge was **superficial**. But of course they would want someone **conversant** with the art publications she was supposed to sell! Why had she even considered applying for this job? She felt herself blushing with **chagrin**. The interview seemed to end all too quickly. Scott Harper assured her Grainger would be in touch. No, they won't, she thought sadly.

HER KNOWLEDGE WAS SUPERFICIAL

THE INTERVIEW PROVED INTIMIDATING

As she made the **trek** back across town, she promised herself to forget Grainger and press on, **undeterred**, to find another job. She'd seen a few possibilities online. She'd just swallow her disappointment, **persevere**, and wait for something to **materialize**. And try to ignore the beat going on in Gwen's room. She sighed.

Her cell phone rang. **Incredulous**, she saw "Grainger" on her caller ID. "Daphne, Scott Harper here. Would you be able to come back, say, in an hour?" His voice was **noncommittal**, but his words caused her to **suppress** a smile. In 15 minutes, if he wanted! Then she knitted her brow in **perplexity**. Why was he calling? Had she dreamed this?

At Grainger, Scott Harper confirmed the reality of the call. "We're expanding," he said. "I'm going to need help. I picked up immediately on your excellent **intuition** and people skills. I want you as my associate in human resources. I just needed to run it by my boss. When I **advocated** for you, she was enthusiastic." He named a good salary and generous benefits. The rest was a blur of paperwork and introductions.

As she headed toward home, both her career and domestic problems solved at once, Daphne was happy to **meditate** on her soon-to-be-silent apartment and thanked her lucky stars.

Daphne's Words, 1st Third

dissonance (DISS·uh·nunce) Discord; the opposite of harmony. Meaning no disrespect to ACDC fans, some people, like Daphne, experience the music in this way, as a clashing of disharmonious musical chords. By extension, dissonance can be used figuratively to indicate any lack of agreement, clash of wills, or gap between beliefs and actions, often referred to as cognitive dissonance. If I save all my vegetable peelings for compost, but I use and toss out 40 plastic bags a day to sit in the landfill, that's cognitive dissonance. (I don't.)

massive (MASS·iv) Large, bulky, heavy, enormous. Think of a *mass*. Or massive mastodons, those old-fashioned elephants from the Stone Age. The music has given Daphne a king-sized headache. You can use the adverb in figurative speech: She was *massively* inconvenienced by the movers, who arrived two days late.

alacrity (a·LAK·krih·tee) Promptness; speed; ready willingness. Note that when you do something with alacrity, you are usually up for it, glad to do it: Gwen is good-natured about agreeing, though she never follows through. If you offer me peppermint ice cream with chocolate sauce, I accept with alacrity, because I love it. If you are asked to vacuum the living room, you may agree to do it promptly, but perhaps not with alacrity.

infuriating (in·FYOOR·ee·ate´·ing) A useful word, meaning maddening or causing fury. To infuriate someone is to put that person in a rage. Taking Tad's forgotten lunchbox to him at school three days running was *infuriating*. We sense that Daphne's biting down on her anger to keep the peace, but she's infuriated because Gwen's behavior is, in fact, infuriating.

mundane (mun·DANE) Ordinary; unimaginative; nothing special. Daphne's job is nothing out of the ordinary. The word carries an implication of monotony and boredom; you're not likely to be thrilled by a mundane commute, for example. The word comes from the Latin word for world and can also be used to characterize earthly or worldly things as opposed to spiritual things: mundane activities versus sacred rituals, for example.

enable (en·AYE·bl) To make possible. A simple operation will *enable* me to use my little finger again. Selling the boat will *enable* us to put Harold through a year of kindergarten. You may have heard the word *enabler* used disapprovingly to describe someone—often a spouse—who abets or encourages someone in negative behaviors such as alcohol and abuse. That person is said to be enabling the behavior. But the word enable can simply mean to provide means or opportunity.

illusory (ih·LOO·serr·ee, ih·LOO-zerr·ee) Seeming but not real; figmentary, deceiving; an illusion. My dream of marrying Madeleine was *illusory*, as she loved someone else. Daphne's privacy is illusory—that is, it doesn't exist in the tiny apartment. Compare *elusive*, page 12, with the same root but a different meaning.

reflecting (rih·FLEK·ting) You know this word in the sense of giving back an image: The sun *reflects* off the water, I see myself *reflected* in the mirror, the child's behavior *reflects* the parents' teaching. The verb to reflect can also mean calmly thinking, going over something in one's mind. And it can mean commenting on these reflections: "I can't stay here," June *reflected*.

ruefully (ROO·full·ee) With regret; also with sorrow or pity, but today we use the word mainly to mean *regretfully*: I lost it all in Las Vegas, he said *ruefully*. Note that if I am rueful, I'm generally calm and philosophical about my problem—accepting it rather than frantically searching for a solution.

impulsively (im·PUL·siv·lee) Without forethought; on a whim; doing what you feel like rather than weighing the pros and cons: "Come to Saratoga with us!" she cried *impulsively*. People with attention deficit hyperactivity disorder often act impulsively. Daphne acted on an impulse she now clearly regrets.

casual (KA·zhu·ull) Superficially, it can be applied to a friend, like Gwen, or to an attitude: a *casual* interest in abstract art. Casual can also mean happening infrequently or by chance: Jesse made *casual* visits to the nursing home. You may also know the word in the sense of informal: *casual* dress, a *casual* dinner.

predilections (preh´·duh·LEK·shuns) A predilection is a liking for, interest in, or predisposition toward something: Gwen is predisposed to favor ACDC. Her predilections in the area of popular music are not shared by Daphne. I have a strong *predilection* for staying home nowadays, as opposed to being robbed and insulted by the airlines.

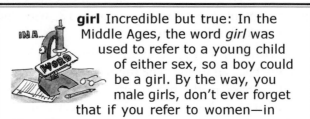

girl Incredible but true: In the Middle Ages, the word *girl* was used to refer to a young child of either sex, so a boy could be a girl. By the way, you male girls, don't ever forget that if you refer to women—in the office, for example—as girls, you must also refer to the men as boys. Quickly, before the industrial-size water-cooler bottle comes down on your head.

✸ PRACTICING DAPHNE'S WORDS, 1ST THIRD

The words for the first third of Daphne's story are:

alacrity	illusory	mundane
casual	impulsively	predilections
dissonance	infuriating	reflecting
enable	massive	ruefully

A. Fill in the blanks with the correct list words.

1. Dolores thought _____ that she had never had a home of her own.

2. Taking chemistry in summer school will _____ me to finish college in August.

3. Being a nurse unfortunately involves many _____ chores, including paperwork.

   4. It was _____ to watch that mean bully score
      14 points.
   5. _____ I said, "Stay and have dinner with us."
B. What list word would cause problems in a choir or
   singing group?
C. Careful is to patience as prompt is to _____.
D. Which list word is the closest synonym for *preferences*?
E. Match the list words with their correct definitions in the
   right-hand column.

   1. casual   a. engaged in contemplation
   2. illusory   b. gigantic
   3. massive   c. deceptive or imaginary
   4. reflecting   d. informal

F. Complete the following story with list words.

   Belinda (on the spur of the moment) hurled a pillow at
   Dick's picture with (ready enthusiasm). Happiness was a
   sham, (fictitious). (Thinking it over) (sadly, with regret),
   she knew her (huge) problem was her own fault. Nothing
   could (empower) Dick to love someone fully. She should
   have kept the relationship (superficial). But she'd had to
   fall for him—what a sad, (ordinary) story! It really was too
   (maddening).

Answers
A. 1. ruefully; 2. enable; 3. mundane; 4. infuriating;
   5. Impulsively
B. dissonance
C. alacrity
D. predilections
E. 1. d; 2. c; 3. b; 4. a
F. impulsively; alacrity; illusory; reflecting; ruefully;
   massive; enable; casual; mundane; infuriating

Daphne's Words, 2nd Third

reputable (REH·pyoo·tuh·bl) Well thought of; respected; of good reputation. We'll be staying at a *reputable* bed and breakfast in Grafton. The word's antonym, *dis*reputable, is more fun: Bob's *disreputable* friend Eric wore his baseball cap backward to his big college interview.

commission (kuh·MISH·un) A word with many related definitions. It can mean, as it does here, a fee or percentage paid to an agent or salesperson who brings in a piece of business: The real estate broker may take a 5-percent *commission* for selling your house. A commission can also mean the assigning of a military rank: She received her *commission* as a second lieutenant. The commission of an act means the performance of it: *Commission* of perjury is a serious offense. And it's a verb as well: You may commission, or appoint, or empower, someone to carry out duties as your representative. More? The dictionary has more.

distinct (dih·STINKT) Clear; notable; noticeable: Daphne has sat up and taken notice of the job's possibilities. One might refer to someone's distinct Southern accent. The word also means distinguishable or separate from one another: Cornell's engineering school, as *distinct* from the school of physics.

ineffable (in·EFF·uh·bl) A useful word. Saying a thing is ineffable is much more impressive than saying it's great. Ineffable means so wonderful or so awful (or so anything) that it can't be described in words. Unspeakable: Picture my *ineffable* horror as Janie's doll floated off down the Thames.

initiate (ih·NIH·shee·ate′) To begin; to set going. That's the sense in which it's used here: Gwen will have to set the wheels in motion to get a new place. Initiate can also mean to introduce: We *initiated* Grandma into the fine art of luge shots. And it can mean to make someone a member (as of a club or organization), especially with ritual or ceremony.

attaining (uh·TANE·ing) Achieving; gaining; successfully reaching. When the stock market rallied, I realized my dream of *attaining* financial security. *Attaining* middle age, he dropped all pretense of dieting. The verb is *attain*. Can Dorabelle *attain* a black belt if she doesn't attend the sessions?

trudged (TRUJD) Walked steadily, but perhaps with fatigue or difficulty. The word may carry overtones of discouragement, unlike strode, which is upbeat and purposeful. Having lost his job, the man *trudged* wearily home. Daphne is trudging because walking to the subway isn't very inspiring, and it's raining.

edifice (ED·ih·fiss) A building or structure, especially a large or imposing one: The Great Pyramid is an impressive *edifice*. People who compulsively build houses or put additions on the ones they've got are sometimes said to have edifice complexes. Well, *I* think that's funny.

ascending (a·SEN·ding) Going up. To ascend means to rise, and there are many ways to do so, depending on whether you are smoke, a hill, a bird, a politician, or, like Daphne, a person in an elevator. You can ascend a staircase or a mountain. The word can mean increasing: The worst earthquakes are listed in *ascending* order of magnitude.

auburn (AW·burn) A dark shade of red or reddish brown, usually referring to hair, but many trees turn this color in the fall. It's both a noun (*auburn* is a color I dislike) and an adjective (her *auburn* hair gleamed in the sun). Their house in Hingham was called Auburn Hills.

intimidating (in·TIM·ih·date´·ing) The verb to intimidate means to frighten, threaten, or make timid; hence, intimidating means causing fear. You may find public speaking intimidating. It's not a super-strong word: Going into battle, for example, would be terrifying rather than intimidating.

relative (RELL·uh·tiv) Regarding; in regard; relative to; about. Scott's questions relative to art and photography are simply about them. *Relative* to your question about Will, he's out of work again. Relative can mean compared to something else: the relative peace of Daphne's apartment with Aerosmith instead of ACDC. We ate under an umbrella in *relative* comfort.

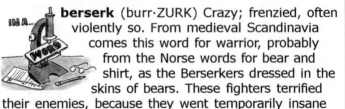

berserk (burr·ZURK) Crazy; frenzied, often violently so. From medieval Scandinavia comes this word for warrior, probably from the Norse words for bear and shirt, as the Berserkers dressed in the skins of bears. These fighters terrified their enemies, because they went temporarily insane and attacked in a frenzy without thought for their own safety. They howled, foamed at the mouth, and bit their shields—an intense state.

☀ PRACTICING DAPHNE'S WORDS, 2ND THIRD

The words for the second third of Daphne's story are:

ascending	distinct	intimidating
attaining	edifice	relative
auburn	ineffable	reputable
commission	initiate	trudged

A. Match the list words with the correct definitions in the right-hand column.

1. attaining   a. plodded wearily
2. commission   b. impressive building
3. edifice   c. fee for bringing in business
4. trudged   d. achieving

B. Was Marilyn Monroe's hair auburn?

C. Which list word is the closest synonym for *begin*?

D. Fill in the blanks with the correct list words.

  1. I took an _____ pleasure in telling Mr. Bigshot his car was totaled.

  2. These are yams, as _____ from sweet potatoes.

  3. There's a dude _____ the staircase.

  4. There's no challenge involved in _____ Dorothy: She's a total cream puff.

E. Which list word is the closest antonym for *absolute*?

F. If I spend the night at a *reputable* motel, I'm likely to

  _____.

  1. stay awake all night   3. have a pleasant stay

  2. be robbed   4. meet shady ladies

G. Complete the following story with list words.

  As I (walked slowly) up the hill in hopes of (reaching) the top by sunset, I saw a strange-looking (building), a (noticeable) gray (compared) to the (reddish brown) autumn leaves, with towers (rising) toward the clouds. It seemed to give off an (indescribable) sense of sadness that was (frightening). Remembering my (duty) to pick up supplies, I was glad to pass by it. There was something not quite (respectable) in its melancholy aura.

Answers

A. 1. d; 2. c; 3. b; 4. a

B. No. (Auburn is reddish-brown.)

C. initiate

D. 1. ineffable; 2. distinct; 3. ascending; 4. intimidating

E. relative

F. 3

G. trudged; attaining; edifice; distinct; relative; auburn; ascending; ineffable; intimidating; commission; reputable

Daphne's Words, 3rd Third

superficial (soo´·per·FISH·ul) On the surface only; lacking in depth. A superficial wound is a shallow wound, not serious; a superficial analysis doesn't get into serious matters. You could say a person who cares only about appearances has superficial values. And Daphne's knowledge of art and photography is superficial: She hasn't studied them in any depth.

conversant (kun·VUR·sunt) Familiar with; knowledgeable about. Daphne quickly realizes she would need to be more conversant with the world of art to be eligible for the job. On the other hand, she's conversant with all the Beatles' lyrics—nobody's all bad. Seriously, this is a useful word: You may be conversant with the rules of the Registry of Motor Vehicles; you may be conversant, or fluent, in French; you may be conversant with sheet metal fabrication.

chagrin (shuh·GRIN) Embarrassment; the way you feel when you fail or are humiliated. Three penalty shots at the basket, and you missed all three: That's chagrin. If you blush, like Daphne, chagrin will make you do it. In French chagrin means sadness or pain. In English it's a verb also, usually used in the passive (to be chagrined): I am *chagrined* to have kept you waiting so long.

trek (TREKK) This word is Africaans, from the Dutch *trekken*, to haul or to migrate. It has come to mean to journey or a journey, especially a long or difficult one: I've had to *trek* all over town to find a top hat you can wear for the cancan number tonight. The Andersons just don't feel like making the *trek* into the city again today.

undeterred (un·dih·TERRD) Not put off; not persuaded not to take a certain action; sticking to one's plan. To deter means to push someone off course, to prevent them from doing something. If you are *un*deterred, you're not letting anything or anybody put you off: There is some evidence serial killers are *undeterred* by the concept of capital punishment.

persevere (per´·suh·VEER) To persist in an activity or way of behaving in spite of obstacles. A person who is undeterred is likely to persevere. A dyslexic person, one who has difficulty reading, must *persevere* in order to decipher the written word. If you persevere, you just keep on keeping on—like the Energizer Bunny, that paragon of perseverance. A fascinating relative of this word is *perseverate*, which means to repeat something insistently or redundantly: In the ambulance, he *perseverated* in asking what had happened to his wife.

materialize (muh·TEER·ee·uh·lyze´) To appear; to arise; to come into existence, especially in a sudden way: The magician waved his wand and a rabbit *materialized*. Daphne is sure something will materialize—that is, show up—on the job front sooner or later.

incredulous (in·KREH·juh·luss) Disbelieving; unable to admit or believe something. Daphne understandably can't believe anyone at Grainger would be calling her; this makes her incredulous. A facial expression or a comment can be incredulous as well as a person: She gave him an *incredulous* sneer. And likely as not, laughed an *incredulous* laugh.

noncommittal (non´·kuh·MITT·ul) Look at the prefix *non-* and the root *commit* and this one's easy: It means not committing oneself, not coming down on either side, not making a clear statement. Scott's tone of voice gives no clue as to his purpose in calling. If you invite me over, I may respond, "Maybe." That's noncommittal.

suppress (suh·PRESS) To put down, restrain, or subdue, by persuasion or force: We *suppressed* the food fight beginning in the dining room. It can also mean, as it does here, to hold one's own emotions or actions in check: Daphne holds back a smile at the thought of her eagerness to return to Grainger. You may suppress a sneeze or a hiccup also. In fact, please do.

perplexity (per·PLEX·ih·tee) Puzzlement. Daphne can't understand why Scott wants to see her again; she is perplexed, or bewildered. The word can apply to a particularly confusing or complicated situation: The plans were a *perplexity*, overwritten with conflicting instructions.

intuition (in´·too·IH·shun) Insight or understanding, and especially the ability to know something instantly without a rational explanation. My *intuition* told me something was wrong inside the building: I grabbed my purse and ran out just as the ceiling collapsed. Women are supposed to be especially good at intuiting, or reading, others' feelings, even when they're unexpressed. I have also known many intuitive men and some women with no intuition at all.

advocated (ADD·voe·kay´·ted) To advocate means to speak in favor of someone or something; to plead the case for or recommend. I can advocate a plan to build a new playground. You might advocate for shorter hours at work. Scott sees Daphne's capabilities and supports hiring her. He is thus an advocate (ADD·vuh·kut) for Daphne.

meditate (MED·ih·tate´) To ponder; to think carefully; to go over in one's mind. She was not inclined to *meditate* on her poor health. I *meditated* on whether to call Johnson back. To meditate can also mean, as you probably know, to put oneself into a condition of deeper spiritual consciousness by breathing exercises or physical activities such as yoga.

✹ PRACTICING DAPHNE'S WORDS, 3RD THIRD

The words for the last third of Daphne's story are:

advocated	materialize	persevere
chagrin	meditate	superficial
conversant	noncommittal	suppressed
incredulous	perplexity	trek
intuition		undeterred

A. If I tell you I made a hole in one, and you don't believe me, you are _____.

    1. conversant   3. noncommittal

    2. incredulous   4. undeterred

B. Fill in the blanks with the correct list words.

    1. Derek really isn't _____ with the Vista operating system.

    2. My _____tells me it's Miss Scarlet in the library with a dagger.

    3. I thought the trip to Mexico would thrill him, but he's _____.

    4. To Theresa's _____, her mother told everyone she's afraid of the dark.

    5. If I _____ long enough, perhaps the ghost of my father will _____.

C. Which sentence uses the word *superficial* correctly?

    1. Don't worry about the cut; it looks bad, but it's a superficial wound.

    2. I was pleased when the spa gave me a superficial skin cleansing.

    3. Superficial boats skim the surface of the water at top speed.

    4. The band had a superficial sound system.

D. Match the list words with their correct definitions in the right-hand column.

    1. perplexity   a. persist despite obstacles

    2. persevere   b. long, weary journey

    3. suppressed   c. puzzlement

    4. trek   d. not put off

    5. undeterred   e. subdued, restrained

E. When senior management met to decide who should be promoted to fill a sudden vacancy, Vanessa spoke glowingly of Arthur's abilities and recommended him for the position; in other words, she _____ for him.

F. Complete the following story with list words.

Kyra was feeling some (embarrassment). The birds and flowers she'd promised on their (difficult journey) had failed to (appear). She paused briefly to (get in touch spiritually), then continued to (keep on) (not changing her course of action). Josie, more (familiar) with the trail than the others, (recommended) turning back. (Disbelieving), Kyra (stifled, held back) a rude response and said, "My (nonrational understanding) tells me we'll see some wonderful views soon. Our discomfort is temporary and (on the surface)." Sure enough, they soon rounded a bend and were surrounded by gorgeous trees and flowers and distant ranges of blue mountains.

Answers

A. 2

B. 1. conversant; 2. intuition; 3. noncommittal; 4. chagrin; 5. meditate; materialize

C. 1

D. 1. c; 2. a; 3. e; 4. b; 5. d

E. advocated

F. chagrin; trek; materialize; meditate; persevere; undeterred; conversant; advocated; Incredulous; suppressed; intuition; superficial

16 *Still More Words You Should Know*

The following four lists include some wonderful words, many used in the SAT. There isn't room to give them the full treatment, with in-depth definitions, examples, related words, and practice exercises, but they too will add a knowledgeable and polished flavor to your speech and writing.

29 Top-Notch Nouns
Know and use these interesting and important nouns!

1. **adversity** (ad·VUR·sih·tee) Misfortune; hard times
2. **amanuensis** (ah·MAN·yoo·EN·siss) One employed to copy manuscripts or take dictation
3. **aversion** (ah·VURR·zhun) Dislike of or fierce opposition to something
4. **candor** (KAN·der) Honesty; frankness
5. **cessation** (sess·AY·shun) Stopping; discontinuance
6. **diffidence** (DIFF·ih·dense) Lack of self-confidence; shyness
7. **diligence** (DIH·lih·jenss) Careful and sustained effort
8. **excerpt** (EK·serpt) A part selected from written or printed matter
9. **finesse** (fih·NESS) Subtle manipulation to gain a point
10. **foliage** (FOE·lee·edj) Growth of leaves

11. **gravity** (GRA·vih·tee) Seriousness

12. **habitant** (HA·bih·tunt) Dweller; resident

13. **impetus** (IM·peh·tuss) Motivator; driving force

14. **insolence** (IN·suh·lenss) Rude, insulting behavior

15. **instigator** (IN·stih·gay´·ter) One who initiates or urges a course of action

16. **integrity** (in·TEH·grih·tee) Uprightness of character and strictness of moral code; wholeness

17. **juncture** (JUNK·chur) An important or critical point in time

18. **lieu** (LYEW) Place; stead (in lieu of means instead of)

19. **microcosm** (MY·kroe·cohz´·um) A system in miniature with analogies to a larger system

20. **minutia** (mih·NOO·shah; mih·NOO-shee-ah; mih·NYOO·shah; mih·NYOO·shee·ah) A small or unimportant detail (plural: minutiae)

21. **nomad** (NOE·mad) One with no fixed home

22. **omniscience** (ahm·NIH·shunss) Infinite knowledge

23. **partisan** (PAR·tih·zun) A supporter or adherent, especially a biased one

24. **proxy** (PROK·zee) Someone authorized to act in place of another

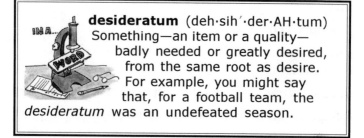

desideratum (deh·sih´·der·AH·tum) Something—an item or a quality— badly needed or greatly desired, from the same root as desire. For example, you might say that, for a football team, the *desideratum* was an undefeated season.

25. **retention** (re·TEN·shun) Keeping or holding in one's possession

26. **solicitude** (soh·LIH·sih·tood´; soh·LIH·sih·tyood´) A state of anxiety or concern, often for another person

27. **truculence** (TRUKK·yoo·lenss) Fierceness; hostility

28. **ultimatum** (ull´·tih·MAY·tum) A final proposal or demand

29. **zenith** (ZEE·nith) Highest point; peak; culmination

29 Top-Notch Verbs

Know and use these verbs to add sparkle to your speaking and writing!

1. **abase** (uh·BASE) To lower in position; to degrade

2. **animadvert** (an´·ih·mad·VERT) To criticize; to comment unfavorably

3. **animate** (AN·ih·mate´) To bring to life

4. **begrudge** (bee·GRUDGE) To covet someone's ownership of

5. **bequeath** (bee·KWEETHE [like *breathe*]; bee·KWEETH [like *teeth*]) To leave to someone in a will

6. **cajole** (kuh·JOLE) To coax or persuade by gentle urging or flattery

7. **collaborate** (kuh·LAB·uh·rate´) To work with others, especially in professional or academic pursuits

8. **concur** (kun·KERR) To agree; to share an opinion

9. **convalesce** (kon´·vuh·LESS) To recover from an illness or medical procedure

10. **corroborate** (kuh·ROB·uh·rate´) To confirm or strengthen with additional evidence

11. **discriminate** (diss·KRIM·ih·nate´) To draw a distinction between items

12. **dominate** (DAH·mih·nate´) To influence; to exercise control over

13. **elapse** (ee·LAPS) To pass, in reference to time

14. **embroil** (em·BROYL) To involve in argument or strife

15. **grimace** (GRIM·uss) To distort one's features, as in pain or revulsion

16. **idealize** (eye·DEE·uh·lyze´) To consider as ideal or perfect

17. **interpolate** (in·TER·puh·late´) To insert new matter between original material or parts

18. **interrogate** (in·TARE·uh·gate´) To examine; to question closely

19. **juxtapose** (JUK·stuh·POZE) To put close together

20. **litigate** (LIT·ih·gate´) To make the subject of a lawsuit

21. **mediate** (MEE·dee·ate´) To negotiate between parties

22. **obviate** (OB·vee·ate´) To make unnecessary; to prevent from happening; to eliminate

23. **pacify** (PASS·ih·fye´) To make peaceful or calm

24. **pulverize** (PUHL·vuh·ryze´) To pound, crush, or grind to powder

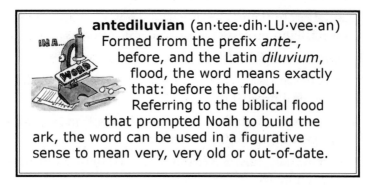

antediluvian (an·tee·dih·LU·vee·an) Formed from the prefix *ante-*, before, and the Latin *diluvium*, flood, the word means exactly that: before the flood. Referring to the biblical flood that prompted Noah to build the ark, the word can be used in a figurative sense to mean very, very old or out-of-date.

25. **quibble** (KWIH·bl) To argue small or inconsequential points

26. **rectify** (REK·tih·fye´) To correct or make right

27. **retrieve** (rih·TREEVE) To bring back; to recover

28. **satiate** (SAY·shee·ate´) To satisfy desire

29. **vindicate** (VINN·dih·kate´) To prove right; to justify

29 Top-Notch Adjectives

Add color to your vocabulary with these adjectives!

1. **adamant** (ADD·uh·munt) Stubbornly unyielding in attitude or opinion

2. **amenable** (uh·MEEN·uh·bl; uh·MEN·uh·bl) Agreeable, open to influence; willing and ready

3. **articulate** (arr·TIK·yuh·lit) Able to express oneself clearly and fluently

4. **astute** (a·STOOT, a·STYOOT) Keen in discernment; clever; ingenious

5. **belligerent** (bel·LIDGE·uh·runt) Inclined to fight; aggressive; hostile

6. **capacious** (cuh·PAY·shuss) Roomy; able to hold a large quantity

7. **cohesive** (koe·HEE·siv) Unified; tending to hold together

8. **congenial** (kun·JEEN·yuhl) Agreeable; suitable; pleasing

9. **explicit** (ek·SPLIH·sit) Clearly spelled out; fully expressed

10. **fitful** (FIT·full) In fits or spells; irregular

11. **hesitant** (HEZ·ih·tunt) Hesitating; undecided; doubtful

12. **infernal** (in·FUR·nuhl) Hellish; devilish; very bothersome or annoying

13. **judicious** (jew·DIH·shuss) Having sound judgment; prudent

14. **laborious** (luh·BORE·ee·uss) Requiring much work or excessive effort; toilsome

15. **monetary** (MON·eh·teh´·ree) Of or pertaining to money

16. **negligent** (NEG·lih·jent) Careless; not attending to what must be done

17. **oblivious** (uh·BLIH·vee·uss) Unaware; unconscious; forgetful

18. **palpable** (PAL·puh·bl) Able to be perceived by feeling or touch

19. **perfidious** (per·FIH·dee·uss) Treacherous; deceitful; given to betraying

20. **prevalent** (PREV·uh·lahnt) Widespread; commonly occurring

21. **querulous** (QUARE·yoo·luss; QUARE-uh-luss) Complaining; discontented; whiny

22. **rigorous** (RIG·uh·russ) Demanding; strict; severe

23. **robust** (roe·BUST) Healthy; powerful; with the strength to endure

24. **sardonic** (sar·DONN·ihk) Scornfully cutting or sarcastic

25. **sedentary** (SEH·den·teh´·ree) Involving much sitting; getting little exercise

26. **terse** (TURSS) Brief and to the point; not wordy

27. **ungainly** (un·GANE·lee) Awkward; clumsy

28. **venerable** (VEN·uh·ruh·bl) Commanding respect because of age or dignity

29. **virulent** (VEER·yuh·lunt; VEER·uh·luhnt) Poisonous or deadly (root: *virus*)

29 Top-Notch Adverbs

Use these handy adverbs to tell how, when, or where something is done.

1. **amply** (AMP·lee) Sufficiently; enough

2. **askance** (uh·SKANSS) Suspiciously; with mistrust

3. **brazenly** (BRAY·zen·lee) Shamelessly or impudently

4. **caustically** (KAW·stih·k[uh]lee) In a sarcastic, critical, stinging manner

5. **conspicuously** (kun·SPIK·yew·uss·lee) Visibly; in a noticeable way

6. **deceitfully** (dih·SEET·full·lee) In a dishonest or corrupt manner

7. **exorbitantly** (ig·ZOR·bih·tunt·ly) Extremely; in a way that exceeds the proper

8. **extemporaneously** (eks·tem·puh·RANE·ee·uss·lee) Without much preparation; off the cuff

9. **fallaciously** (fa·LAY·shuss·lee) Falsely or mistakenly

10. **fatuously** (FAT·chew·uss·lee) Idiotically; foolishly

11. **fervently** (FURR·vent·lee) Intensely; enthusiastically

12. **gratuitously** (gra·TOO·ih·tuss·lee; gra·TYEW·ih·tuss·lee) Voluntarily OR without justification

13. **humanely** (hew·MANE·lee) Kindly; compassionately

14. **ignominiously** (ig·nuh·MINN·ee·uss·lee) Shamefully; in a humiliating manner

15. **innocuously** (in·NOKK·yoo·uss·lee) Harmlessly; inoffensively

16. **jovially** (JOE·vee·uh·lee) In a cheerful or joyous and humorous way

17. **leniently** (LEE·nee·unt·lee, LEEN·yunt·lee) Tolerantly; indulgently

18. **liberally** (LIB·er·uh·lee, LIB·ruh·lee) Freely; generously; abundantly

19. **materially** (muh·TEER·ee·uh·lee) To an important extent; quite a bit

20. **meticulously** (meh·TI·kyuh·luss·lee) Carefully; precisely; in a fussy manner

21. **morosely** (muh·ROESS·lee) Gloomily; in an ill-humored way

22. **optimally** (OP·tuh·muh·lee) In a most favorable or desirable way

23. **prodigiously** (pruh·DIJ·uss·lee) Enormously; greatly; marvelously

24. **prohibitively** (proe·HIB·ih·tiv·lee) Forbiddingly; so much so as to prevent use or purchase

25. **reputedly** (rih·PUTE·ihd·lee) According to general belief; supposedly

26. **verbosely** (vurr·BOSE·lee) In a roundabout, talkative, or wordy manner

27. **vindictively** (vin·DIK·tiv·lee) Revengefully; spitefully

28. **vociferously** (voe·SIFF·uh·russ·lee) In a loud, noisy, uproarious manner

29. **wantonly** (WAHN·tun·lee) Maliciously; recklessly; sexually unrestrainedly

Afterword

Congratulations! You've just added hundreds of new words to your vocabulary. Go out and dazzle the neighbors.

But don't stop now. You can keep adding to your store of words in an easy and pleasant way, simply by *reading*. Read the newspaper, read the classics, read the best-sellers. Read online, hard copy, billboards. Read on the subway, on the plane, in the tub. If you prefer screens to books, use a Kindle. Above all, read. Nothing makes so much difference to your vocabulary. You can almost always figure out the meaning of a word from the context, or your knowledge of prefixes, roots, and suffixes. If not, make a note of it and consult *www.dictionary.com* or the floor-standing model you got as a graduation present.

Another good way to keep building your vocabulary is via the Internet. If you Google "vocabulary," you'll get more than 50 *million* entries. There are Websites offering free tutorials, puzzles, word-a-day features, and heaps more. Though their word definitions aren't usually comprehensive, they're a good start. One of my favorites is *www.freerice.org*, a nonprofit site that takes you through vocabulary quizzes. For each word you get right, the organization donates 20 grains of rice to Third World countries through the United Nations food program. Talk about a win-win! And there are many more excellent programs, so keep going.

I hope you've had fun with *Awesome Vocabulary* and added to your confidence as well as your vocabulary.

Enjoy the new,

word-enabled you!

✳

Appendix:
Your New Vocabulary

au fait (page 128)

auburn (page 179)

audacity (page 52)

autres temps, autres moeurs (page 128)

aversion (page 187)

avert (page 162)

begrudge (page 189)

beguiling (page 119)

belligerent (page 191)

bemused (page 67)

bequeath (page 189)

berserk (page 180)

bibliophile (page 137)

boasted (page 50)

bon appétit (page 128)

bona fide (page 129)

brazenly (page 193)

c'est la vie (page 129)

cajole (page 189)

calculations (page 74)

candor (page 187)

capacious (page 191)

cardiovascular (page 164)

carte blanche (page 129)

casual (page 175)

caustically (page 193)

cessation (page 187)

chagrin (page 182)

chancel (page 125)

chassis (page 48)

chauvinist (page 60)

che sarà, sarà (page 133)

cherchez la femme (page 129)

ciao (page 129)

clamber (page 12)

cohesive (page 191)

collaborate (page 189)

comme il faut (page 129)

commission (page 178)

commonwealth (page 38)

compassion (page 73)

competent (page 67)

comprehend (page 139)

concur (page 189)

conducive (page 96)

confidant (page 69)

congenial (page 191)

consciousness (page 139)

consequently (page 11)

conspicuously (page 193)

consternation (page 166)

constraint (page 119)

contempt (page 91)

contending (page 165)

contrived (page 48)

convalesce (page 189)

conversant (page 182)

converse (page 118)

cordon bleu (page 129)

corroborate (page 189)

countenance (page 159)

cower (page 92)

credit (page 100)

crucial (page 67)

cul-de-sac (page 129)

cyberspace (page 165)

daunting (page 92)

de rigueur (page 130)

deceitfully (page 193)

decimate (page 60)

déjà vu (page 130)

denizens (page 16)

Deo gratias (page 130)

deracinate (page 91)

deranged (page 138)

desideratum (page 188)

despondently (page 162)

diffidence (page 187)

dilemma (page 74)

diligence (page 187)

disciplined (page 71)

disconsolate (page 70)

discriminate (page 189)

disheveled (page 70)

disinclination (page 66)

disinterested (page 60)

dismissive (page 70)

dissonance (page 173)

distinct (page 178)

doleful (page 96)

dominate (page 190)

doppelganger (page 130)

double entendre (page 130)

e.g. (page 130)

edifice (page 179)

eerie (page 162)

egregiously (page 74)

elapse (page 190)

elated (page 55)

electrocute (page 43)

elicited (page 55)

elude (page 12)

emanating (page 92)

emboldened (page 99)

embroil (page 190)

en famille (page 130)

enable (page 174)

encumbered (page 116)

endured (page 146)

engendered (page 142)

enhance (page 56)

ensconced (page 116)

enterprising (page 95)

ephemeral (page 55)

eradicate (page 93)

eroded (page 47)

erudite (page 119)

et cetera (page 130)

et tu, Brute? (page 131)

evaporate (page 57)

eventually (page 17)

exasperation (page 13)

excerpt (page 187)

excised (page 21)

excruciating (page 47)

execute (page 16)

exhilaration (page 158)

exorbitantly (page 193)

expenditures (page 21)

explicit (page 191)

extemporaneously (page 193)

extracting (page 21)

extricate (page 48)

exuded (page 119)

fallaciously (page 193)

fatuously (page 193)

fell swoop (page 100)

felon (page 167)

fervently (page 193)

fiancé/fiancée (page 131)

fiasco (page 34)

filet (page 21)

finesse (page 187)

fitful (page 191)

flabbergasted (page 13)

flailing (page 18)

foliage (page 187)

folie à deux (page 131)

fortuitous (page 100)

frantically (page 17)

frivolity (page 120)

fulsome (page 60)

futile (page 51)

gallant (page 17)

gauge (page 166)

ghastly (page 146)

giddy (page 158)

gingerly (page 47)

girl (page 176)

grande dame (page 131)

gratuitously (page 193)

gravity (page 188)

grimace (page 190)

gyrate (page 17)

habitant (page 188)

hailed (page 115)

harassment (page 73)

harbinger (page 101)

hasta la vista (page 131)

hesitant (page 191)

hitherto (page 138)

honi soit qui mal y pense (page 131)

hors de combat (page 132)

hors d'oeuvre (page 132)

hover (page 47)

humanely (page 193)

hunkered (page 20)

i.e. (page 132)

idealize (page 190)

ignominiously (page 193)

illusory (page 175)

illustrious (page 142)

immediate (page 71)

impair (page 95)

impeccably (page 95)

impelled (page 75)

impervious (page 161)

impetus (page 188)

imploded (page 162)

imposing (page 56)

impulsively (page 175)

in medias res (page 132)

inaccessible (page 145)

inappropriate (page 70)

incoherently (page 92)

incredulous (page 183)

incredulously (page 74)

indispensable (page 92)

indolent (page 69)

indubitably (page 138)

ineffable (page 178)

infamous (page 61)

infatuated (page 115)

infernal (page 191)

inflammable (page 61)

infra dig (page 132)

infuriating (page 174)

initiate (page 178)

innocuously (page 193)

inopportunely (page 55)

inshallah (page 132)

insolence (page 188)

instigator (page 188)

integrity (page 188)

interim (page 115)

interpolate (page 190)

interrogate (page 190)

intimidating (page 179)

intolerable (page 124)

intuition (page 184)

invaluable (page 61)

inveigle (page 15)

invincible (page 161)

iota (page 147)

iridescent (page 18)

jaunty (page 51)

je ne sais quoi (page 133)

jell (page 66)

jovially (page 193)

judicious (page 192)

juncture (page 188)

juxtapose (page 190)

kilter (page 142)

Kinder, Kirche, Kuche (page 133)

laborious (page 192)

labyrinth (page 116)

latent (page 120)

leniently (page 194)

liberally (page 194)

lieu (page 188)

lingering (page 66)

lithe (page 99)

litigate (page 190)

lounged (page 158)

MacGuffin (page 69)

maintain (page 16)

massive (page 174)

materialize (page 183)

materially (page 194)

mediate (page 190)

meditate (page 184)

merits (page 165)

metamorphosis (page 22)

meticulously (page 194)
microcosm (page 188)
minuscule (page 99)
minutia (page 188)
miscalculation (page 96)
modish (page 99)
momentous (page 123)
monetary (page 192)
morosely (page 194)
morph (page 100)
mortifying (page 117)
mundane (page 174)
mustered (page 18)
mute (page 20)
mystified (page 120)
negligent (page 192)
negotiated (page 166)
noisome (page 61)
nomad (page 188)
nonchalant (page 100)
noncommittal (page 183)
nonplussed (page 61)
nota bene (page 133)
notorious (page 52)
nuance (page 133)
oblivious (page 192)
observed (page 67)
obsessed (page 138)
obviate (page 190)
ominous (page 48)
omniscience (page 188)
opined (page 145)

optimally (page 194)
ordeal (page 146)
ostracize (page 91)
pacify (page 190)
palpable (page 192)
paramount (page 51)
partisan (page 188)
peccadillo (page 73)
peculiar (page 141)
penultimate (page 62)
perceive (page 158)
perfidious (page 192)
perplexity (page 184)
persevere (page 183)
perusal (page 137)
perverse (page 66)
plausible (page 62)
potential (page 74)
preceded (page 70)
predicament (page 73)
predilections (page 176)
prevalent (page 192)
proclaimed (page 49)
prodigiously (page 194)
profound (page 12)
prohibitively (page 194)
prompt (page 96)
proscribed (page 56)
providentially (page 48)
proximity (page 54)
proxy (page 188)
pseudonym (page 93)

pulverize (page 190)
que sera, sera (page 133)
quell (page 123)
querulous (page 192)
quibble (page 191)
rapture (page 124)
ravenous (page 51)
recede (page 115)
reckoned (page 116)
recoil (page 141)
recollected (page 146)
recourse (page 71)
rectify (page 191)
reflecting (page 175)
reflexively (page 163)
refrain (page 123)
reiterate (page 166)
relative (page 180)
reluctant (page 11)
remorse (page 163)
replica (page 124)
repressed (page 145)
reputable (page 178)
reputedly (page 194)
resounding (page 22)
restrain (page 99)
retention (page 189)
retrieve (page 191)
retrospect (page 51)
revealed (page 157)
revive (page 146)
rhetorically (page 13)

rigorous (page 192)
robust (page 192)
ruefully (page 175)
rummage (page 56)
sardonic (page 192)
satiate (page 191)
schadenfraude (page 134)
scintilla (page 120)
scrutiny (page 157)
sedentary (page 192)
seduce (page 11)
self-assured (page 95)
serenity (page 120)
simmering (page 74)
solicitude (page 189)
soporific (page 124)
strode (page 22)
subconscious (page 66)
subside (page 97)
substantial (page 158)
sultry (page 51)
supercilious (page 147)
superficial (page 182)
suppressed (page 183)
surmount (page 162)
syndrome (page 145)
teemed (page 95)
tension (page 16)
tepidly (page 159)
terse (page 192)
thrashing (page 12)
throng (page 142)

thug (page 137)
thunderstruck (page 166)
tier (page 124)
transformed (page 22)
transient (page 159)
transpiring (page 138)
trauma (page 145)
traverse (page 65)
trek (page 182)
truculence (page 189)
trudged (page 179)
tumultuous (page 123)
ultimately (page 143)
ultimatum (page 189)
undeterred (page 182)
ungainly (page 192)
unkempt (page 91)
untoward (page 141)
utter (page 12)
vast (page 52)
venerable (page 192)

verbosely (page 194)
verge (page 65)
verified (page 55)
vexed (page 142)
vindicate (page 191)
vindictively (page 194)
virulent (page 192)
visceral (page 55)
vivacious (page 141)
vociferously (page 194)
void (page 165)
vulnerable (page 162)
wantonly (page 194)
wistfully (page 96)
wunderkind (page 134)
yielded (page 138)
zeitgeist (page 134)
zenith (page 189)
zephyr (page 13)

Index

About the Author

BECKY BURCKMYER has enjoyed a lifelong (well, not yet) fascination with the English language, ever since a Eureka moment involving the derivation of the word tricycle. Raised in Virginia in a family that cares passionately about language (poetry, correct grammar, words in all contexts), she graduated from Wellesley College with a BA in English and earned her MS in Library Science from Simmons College.

For more than 20 years Becky has consulted on various aspects of writing, as a writer, copy editor, one-on-one writing coach, and seminar leader. She designed and taught a number of courses for middle and upper-level management, including Business Writing for Senior Managers, Responding to Customer Complaints, and E-Mail Etiquette at Work. She has worked primarily with customers in the greater Boston area, such as Analog Devices, Eastern Bank, Fidelity Investments, Fleet Financial Services, John Hancock, and the National Association of Independent Schools. She has written innumerable articles for in-house newsletters for the banking and insurance industry as well as for some major newspapers and minor magazines. She has also served as copy editor for countless quarterly and annual reports, magazines, corporate newsletters, and full-length books. Becky's *Why Does My Boss Hate My Writing?* was published by Adams Media and published subsequently by Barnes & Noble.

Twenty-odd years of dealing with incorrect writing has only increased her sense of the importance of expressing oneself with scrupulous accuracy.

Becky lives with her husband, Larry, in Marblehead, Massachusetts. Besides finding fault with other people's copy, Becky's interests include reading (she's belonged to the same book club for 34 years), opera, sailing, beachcombing, and family.